# REMOTE SENSING TECHNOLOGY FOR ARCHAEOLOGICAL EXPLORATION

Shah Rukh

# CONTENTS

# CHAPTER 1: INTRODUCTION TO REMOTE SENSING IN ARCHAEOLOGY

Remote sensing is a powerful and versatile technology that has revolutionized the field of archaeology over the past few decades. This interdisciplinary approach involves the collection and interpretation of data from a distance, typically through the use of various sensors, instruments, and technologies. In the context of archaeology, remote sensing provides a non-invasive means to discover, map, and analyze archaeological sites and features, often hidden beneath the earth's surface. This comprehensive introduction will explore the fundamental principles, techniques, and applications of remote sensing in archaeology, shedding light on how this methodology has transformed the way we study and understand our past.

**I. Understanding Remote Sensing:**

A. **Definition and Overview:** Remote sensing encompasses a wide array of techniques that allow archaeologists to collect data without direct physical contact with the target area. It relies on the interaction between electromagnetic radiation and the Earth's surface to gather information. These methods enable researchers to explore landscapes, identify archaeological sites, and monitor changes in the environment over time. There are several key elements that underpin the field of remote sensing in archaeology:

    1. **Electromagnetic Spectrum:** Remote sensing utilizes different parts of the electromagnetic spectrum, such as visible light, infrared, microwave, and radar, to capture information. Each portion of the spectrum has specific applications and can reveal distinct aspects of

archaeological sites.

2. **Sensors and Platforms:** Various instruments are used to capture data, including satellites, drones, airborne cameras, ground-based instruments, and even handheld devices. The choice of sensor and platform depends on the specific goals of the archaeological investigation.

3. **Data Processing and Analysis:** Remote sensing data often require extensive processing and analysis, including image enhancement, feature extraction, and geospatial mapping. These techniques help archaeologists interpret the information effectively.

B. **Advantages of Remote Sensing in Archaeology:**

1. **Non-Invasive:** One of the primary advantages of remote sensing is that it does not require physical excavation. This non-invasive approach is particularly useful for preserving archaeological sites and their cultural heritage.

2. **Wide Coverage:** Remote sensing allows for the rapid and large-scale exploration of landscapes, making it possible to identify potential archaeological features over vast areas in a short period.

3. **Multi-Temporal Analysis:** Repeated remote sensing surveys can track changes in archaeological sites and monitor threats such as looting, erosion, or land development over time.

4. **Multi-Scale Analysis:** Archaeologists can use remote sensing to investigate sites at various scales, from regional landscapes to individual structures or artifacts.

**II. Techniques in Remote Sensing for Archaeology:**

A. **Aerial Photography:** Historically, aerial photography was one of the earliest forms of remote sensing in archaeology. It involves capturing high-resolution images of the Earth's surface from aircraft or satellites. Aerial photographs can reveal ancient field systems, crop marks, and other subtle surface features that may indicate the presence of buried archaeological sites.

B. **LiDAR (Light Detection and Ranging):** LiDAR is a technology that uses laser pulses to measure the distance between the sensor and the Earth's surface. It can create detailed three-dimensional models of the terrain, allowing archaeologists to detect subtle elevation variations, hidden structures, and ancient road networks.

C. **Satellite Imagery:** Satellites equipped with various sensors provide a valuable source of data for archaeologists. They can capture multispectral images, which reveal different aspects of the landscape, such as vegetation patterns, soil variations, and land use changes, helping identify potential archaeological sites.

D. **Thermal Infrared Imaging:** Thermal infrared cameras can detect variations in surface temperature, revealing subsurface features like buried walls and structures. This technique is especially useful for identifying subsurface ruins or buried architectural elements.

E. **Ground-Penetrating Radar (GPR):** GPR is a ground-based technique that uses radar waves to penetrate the ground and detect buried features. It can reveal subsurface anomalies, such as walls, foundations, or buried artifacts, without excavation.

F. **Magnetometry:** Magnetometry involves measuring variations in the Earth's magnetic field. It is highly effective in detecting archaeological features with a contrast in magnetic properties, such as hearths, kilns, or iron artifacts.

G. **Electrical Resistance Survey:** This method measures the electrical resistance of the ground, which can help identify buried features like ditches, walls, and occupation layers. Variations in resistance indicate subsurface archaeological anomalies.

**III. Applications of Remote Sensing in Archaeology:**

A. **Site Detection and Mapping:** Remote sensing techniques help identify and map archaeological sites, including buried cities, settlements, and burial mounds. These methods are particularly useful in areas where dense vegetation or urban development conceals archaeological features.

B. **Cultural Heritage Preservation:** Remote sensing aids in monitoring the condition of archaeological sites and heritage assets. It helps safeguard cultural heritage by identifying threats such as land degradation, looting, or natural disasters.

C. **Landscape Archaeology:** Researchers use remote sensing to study ancient landscapes, track changes in land use, and identify ancient transportation networks, such as roads, canals, and trade routes.

D. **Environmental Archaeology:** Archaeologists utilize remote sensing to investigate how past human societies adapted to and influenced their environments. This includes studying changes in vegetation, water management systems, and agriculture.

E. **Predictive Modeling:** Remote sensing data can be used to develop predictive models for archaeological site locations. By analyzing the landscape's features, archaeologists can identify areas most likely to contain archaeological remains.

**IV. Challenges and Future Directions:**

A. **Data Interpretation and Integration:** Interpreting remote sensing data in archaeology can be complex and requires expertise. Integrating data from multiple sensors and platforms is a challenge that archaeologists continue to face.

B. **Data Access and Cost:** Access to high-quality remote sensing data can be costly, and researchers often need to collaborate with government agencies or commercial providers. Balancing the cost of data acquisition with the potential benefits is an ongoing concern.

C. **Environmental Factors:** Environmental conditions, such as weather and vegetation cover, can affect the quality and availability of remote sensing data, requiring careful planning and data correction.

D. **Ethical and Cultural Considerations:** Archaeologists must consider the ethical implications of remote sensing, including the impact on local communities and cultural heritage. Balancing scientific goals with cultural preservation is essential.

The field of remote sensing in archaeology continues to evolve rapidly, with advancements in technology and analytical methods. As our understanding of remote sensing techniques deepens, we can expect even greater contributions to our knowledge of the past and the preservation of our cultural heritage. The non-invasive, wide-scale, and multi-temporal nature of remote sensing makes it an indispensable tool for archaeologists seeking to uncover the mysteries of ancient civilizations and landscapes. It is a testament to the enduring synergy between science and history, pushing the boundaries of what we know about our shared human heritage.

# CHAPTER 2: HISTORICAL PERSPECTIVES ON REMOTE SENSING IN ARCHAEOLOGY

The use of remote sensing in archaeology represents a fascinating intersection of technology and history, as it has transformed the way archaeologists explore, document, and understand the past. This comprehensive exploration of the historical perspectives on remote sensing in archaeology will delve into the evolution of this field, tracking the development of technologies and methodologies that have brought archaeologists closer to uncovering the mysteries of ancient civilizations.

**I. Early Antecedents:**

A. **Aerial Photography in the Early 20th Century:** The roots of remote sensing in archaeology can be traced back to the early 20th century when aerial photography emerged as a powerful tool. Archaeologists, such as O.G.S. Crawford, recognized the potential of capturing images from above to reveal hidden archaeological features. Aerial photographs taken during World War I and II inadvertently unveiled crop marks and other surface features, leading to the discovery of numerous archaeological sites in the United Kingdom, notably the famous Nazca Lines in Peru.

B. **The Emergence of Satellite Imagery:** The 1960s saw the launch of Earth-observing satellites like Landsat. These satellites captured images of the Earth's surface in various wavelengths, including visible and infrared light. Archaeologists quickly grasped the potential of satellite imagery to detect surface features not visible from the ground, and this marked the beginning of modern remote sensing in archaeology.

## II. Advancements in Technology:

A. **Development of Airborne Sensors:** As technology advanced, airborne sensors and cameras became more sophisticated. Archaeologists could now obtain high-resolution images and multispectral data that provided valuable insights into vegetation patterns, soil types, and the presence of archaeological features beneath the surface.

B. **Introduction of LiDAR Technology:** LiDAR, a revolutionary technology that employs laser pulses to measure the Earth's surface with remarkable accuracy, became a game-changer for archaeological research. It was initially used for topographic mapping but soon found applications in archaeology. LiDAR has unveiled hidden landscapes, such as ancient Maya cities hidden beneath the Central American rainforests and Roman roads in the British countryside.

C. **Enhanced Satellite Capabilities:** Satellite technology continued to evolve, with the launch of high-resolution imaging satellites like IKONOS and QuickBird. These satellites allowed archaeologists to capture detailed images of archaeological sites and features from space, further expanding the scope of remote sensing applications.

D. **Development of Ground-Based Sensors:** Technological innovations also extended to ground-based sensors, such as ground-penetrating radar (GPR) and magnetometers, which became invaluable tools for non-invasive subsurface investigations. GPR, for instance, enabled the detection of buried structures and artifacts without excavation.

## III. Remote Sensing Applications:

A. **Discovering Hidden Cities and Settlements:** Remote sensing has played a pivotal role in the discovery of hidden cities and settlements worldwide. The use of satellite imagery, aerial photography, and LiDAR has led to the identification of ancient

Mayan cities, Angkor Wat in Cambodia, and numerous Roman and medieval sites in Europe.

B. **Monitoring Environmental Changes:** Archaeologists have employed remote sensing to monitor the impact of environmental changes on archaeological sites. Rising sea levels, climate change, and human activities pose threats to cultural heritage, and remote sensing aids in tracking these changes.

C. **Predictive Modeling:** The accumulation of remote sensing data has facilitated predictive modeling, allowing archaeologists to identify potential site locations based on landscape features. This approach has been especially useful in cultural resource management and archaeological survey planning.

D. **Cultural Heritage Preservation:** Remote sensing technology assists in cultural heritage preservation by documenting and monitoring sites threatened by looting, urban development, or natural disasters. It helps to prioritize and implement conservation efforts.

**IV. Challenges and Ethical Considerations:**

A. **Data Accessibility:** While technology has advanced, accessing high-quality remote sensing data can still be challenging due to cost and data-sharing restrictions. Collaborations with governments, institutions, and commercial providers are often necessary.

B. **Interpretation and Expertise:** Interpreting remote sensing data requires expertise and training. Archaeologists must be proficient in data analysis and image processing to extract meaningful information accurately.

C. **Ethical Considerations:** Archaeologists and remote sensing specialists must navigate ethical concerns, such as the impact of remote sensing on local communities, cultural heritage preservation, and the balance between scientific exploration and cultural sensitivity.

**V. Future Directions:**

A. **Integration of Multiple Data Sources:** The future of remote sensing in archaeology lies in the integration of data from various sources, such as satellite imagery, LiDAR, GPR, and environmental sensors, to create comprehensive archaeological models.

B. **Advancements in Machine Learning:** Machine learning and artificial intelligence will play a significant role in automating the analysis of remote sensing data, making it more accessible and efficient.

C. **Enhanced Resolution and Sensors:** Continued advancements in sensor technology will result in even higher-resolution data, enabling archaeologists to uncover finer details of archaeological sites and features.

D. **Community Involvement:** Future directions also include involving local communities in remote sensing projects, respecting their heritage and involving them in the decision-making processes regarding site preservation and exploration.

In summary, the historical perspectives on remote sensing in archaeology demonstrate a remarkable journey from the early days of aerial photography to the present, where advanced technologies like LiDAR and high-resolution satellite imagery have transformed the field. The applications of remote sensing in archaeology continue to evolve, and with ongoing technological advancements and ethical considerations, the future of this interdisciplinary approach holds great promise for uncovering the secrets of our ancient past while ensuring the preservation of cultural heritage for generations to come.

# CHAPTER 3: PRINCIPLES OF REMOTE SENSING TECHNOLOGY

Remote sensing technology is a critical tool for gathering information about the Earth's surface and its various features from a distance. This interdisciplinary field combines elements of physics, engineering, and data science to acquire and interpret data using sensors and instruments mounted on satellites, aircraft, drones, or ground-based platforms. Understanding the principles of remote sensing technology is fundamental for a wide range of applications, including environmental monitoring, disaster management, agriculture, forestry, urban planning, and, of course, archaeology and earth sciences.

## I. The Electromagnetic Spectrum:

A. **Definition:** The electromagnetic spectrum consists of all the different wavelengths of electromagnetic radiation, ranging from high-energy, short-wavelength gamma rays and X-rays to longer-wavelength ultraviolet, visible light, and even longer radio waves and microwaves. Remote sensing technology leverages various parts of this spectrum to gather information.

B. **Interaction with Earth's Surface:** Different wavelengths interact with the Earth's surface in distinct ways. For instance, visible light is reflected by objects, while microwaves can penetrate the ground and bounce back, providing information about subsurface features. Understanding these interactions is crucial for remote sensing applications.

## II. The Remote Sensing Process:

A. **Energy Source:** The remote sensing process typically begins with an energy source that emits electromagnetic radiation, such as sunlight, radar, or laser pulses. This radiation is directed towards the Earth's surface.

B. **Interaction with Target:** As the energy source reaches the Earth's surface, it interacts with the target or feature of interest. This interaction causes some of the energy to be absorbed, some to be reflected, and some to be transmitted, depending on the nature of the target material.

C. **Sensor or Detector:** A sensor or detector, which can be on a satellite, an aircraft, or a ground-based platform, collects the energy that is reflected or emitted by the Earth's surface. The sensor records the data, which is in the form of digital images or other measurements.

D. **Data Transmission and Storage:** The collected data is then transmitted to a ground station or stored for further analysis. This data can be in various forms, including multispectral or hyperspectral images, LiDAR point clouds, radar data, or thermal infrared measurements.

E. **Data Processing and Analysis:** Once the data is received, it undergoes extensive processing and analysis. This involves calibration, correction, and enhancement of the data to ensure its accuracy and usefulness for specific applications.

F. **Interpretation and Decision-Making:** Remote sensing experts and scientists interpret the processed data to extract information about the Earth's surface, including land cover, land use, temperature, elevation, and more. This information is then used for decision-making, research, or policy development.

**III. Types of Remote Sensing:**

A. **Passive Remote Sensing:** In passive remote sensing, sensors detect naturally occurring electromagnetic radiation, such as sunlight, and measure the energy reflected or emitted by the Earth's surface. The most common example is visible and infrared imagery captured by satellites.

B. **Active Remote Sensing:** Active remote sensing involves sensors that emit their own energy and measure the return signal. Radar and LiDAR are examples of active remote sensing technologies. Radar sends microwave signals and records the signals that bounce back, while LiDAR uses laser pulses and measures the time it takes for the pulses to return.

## IV. Sensors and Platforms:

A. **Satellites:** Satellites are the most commonly used platforms for remote sensing. They offer global coverage and a range of sensors for various applications. Examples include Landsat for Earth observation, and Sentinel satellites for environmental monitoring.

B. **Aircraft:** Aircraft are often used for higher-resolution remote sensing applications. These platforms can carry a variety of sensors, and they are particularly useful for aerial photography, hyperspectral imaging, and LiDAR surveys.

C. **Drones (Unmanned Aerial Vehicles - UAVs):** Drones are flexible and cost-effective platforms for remote sensing. They can capture high-resolution imagery and are used for applications like precision agriculture, forestry, and infrastructure inspection.

D. **Ground-Based Sensors:** Ground-based sensors are used for local-scale observations. These may include weather stations, soil moisture sensors, and ground-penetrating radar systems, among others.

## V. Types of Remote Sensing Data:

A. **Multispectral and Hyperspectral Data:** Multispectral data capture a few specific wavelengths within the electromagnetic spectrum, typically divided into several bands. Hyperspectral data, on the other hand, capture many narrow and contiguous bands, allowing for highly detailed spectral analysis.

B. **LiDAR Data:** LiDAR data provide detailed three-dimensional information about the Earth's surface. It is particularly useful for generating high-resolution digital elevation models and detecting subtle terrain features.

C. **Radar Data:** Radar data are used for all-weather, day-and-night imaging. They can penetrate vegetation and clouds, making them valuable for various applications, including agriculture, forestry, and disaster monitoring.

D. **Thermal Infrared Data:** Thermal infrared data measure the heat emitted by objects. They are useful for applications such as temperature monitoring, environmental analysis, and building energy assessments.

## VI. Applications of Remote Sensing Technology:

A. **Environmental Monitoring:** Remote sensing plays a crucial role in tracking environmental changes, including deforestation, glacier melt, and land cover changes. It aids in assessing the impact of climate change on ecosystems.

B. **Agriculture and Precision Farming:** Farmers use remote sensing to monitor crop health, optimize irrigation, and detect pest outbreaks. It enables precision agriculture practices, improving crop yield and resource efficiency.

C. **Forestry Management:** LiDAR and multispectral data are employed to monitor forest health, measure tree height, estimate biomass, and plan sustainable forestry practices.

D. **Urban Planning and Infrastructure Management:** Remote sensing is used to monitor urban expansion, plan transportation networks, and assess infrastructure health. It aids in disaster management and urban development.

E. **Disaster Management:** Remote sensing technology provides rapid response capabilities for monitoring natural disasters such as earthquakes, floods, wildfires, and hurricanes. It aids in damage assessment and emergency response planning.

F. **Archaeology and Cultural Heritage Preservation:** In archaeology, remote sensing is utilized to discover hidden archaeological features, monitor sites, and plan excavations. It helps preserve cultural heritage by identifying and protecting ancient structures.

G. **Geological and Geophysical Surveys:** LiDAR, radar, and multispectral data assist in geological and geophysical surveys for mineral exploration, fault analysis, and the assessment of geohazards.

H. **Climate Studies:** Remote sensing is instrumental in climate studies, providing data on temperature, sea level rise, and atmospheric conditions. It contributes to our understanding of climate change.

I. **Oceanography and Coastal Monitoring:** Remote sensing technology is employed to study ocean currents, sea surface temperature, and coastal changes. It helps manage fisheries, monitor oil spills, and study marine ecosystems.

**VII. Challenges and Future Developments:**

A. **Data Management and Big Data:** The vast amount of data generated by remote sensing requires efficient data management and storage solutions. The growth of big data in remote sensing necessitates advances in data processing and analysis techniques.

B. **Resolution and Sensor Technology:** Improvements in sensor technology will lead to higher spatial and spectral resolutions, enabling more detailed and accurate observations.

C. **Artificial Intelligence and Machine Learning:** Machine learning and artificial intelligence will play a significant role in automating data analysis, pattern recognition, and information extraction from remote sensing data.

D. **Global Collaboration:** Global collaboration is crucial for sharing data, especially for environmental and climate monitoring. International partnerships are essential for addressing global challenges.

In conclusion, the principles of remote sensing technology are firmly rooted in the physics of electromagnetic radiation and the engineering of sensors and platforms. Remote sensing has a wide array of applications, from environmental monitoring to disaster management and archaeology, providing valuable insights into our planet's dynamics and human history. As technology continues to evolve and global challenges become increasingly pressing, remote sensing will play a central role in helping us understand and address complex issues, making it a dynamic and critical field in the 21st century.

# CHAPTER 4: SATELLITE-BASED REMOTE SENSING IN ARCHAEOLOGY

Satellite-based remote sensing has revolutionized the field of archaeology, enabling researchers to explore and study archaeological sites and landscapes in a non-invasive and efficient manner. This technology has proven invaluable for identifying hidden archaeological features, monitoring site preservation, and conducting large-scale surveys. In this comprehensive exploration of satellite-based remote sensing in archaeology, we will delve into the fundamental principles, the technology behind it, its applications, and the transformative impact it has had on archaeological research.

## I. Fundamental Principles:

A. **Satellite Imaging and the Electromagnetic Spectrum:** Satellite-based remote sensing leverages the electromagnetic spectrum to capture images and data from Earth's surface. Different wavelengths of electromagnetic radiation, including visible light, infrared, and microwave, interact with the Earth's surface in unique ways, allowing archaeologists to glean information about buried archaeological features and the landscape.

B. **Interaction of Satellite Sensors:** Satellite sensors, positioned in low Earth orbit (LEO) or geostationary orbit, capture electromagnetic radiation emitted or reflected by the Earth's surface. The sensors are equipped with various spectral bands, each sensitive to a specific wavelength, enabling the measurement of surface properties such as vegetation health, land cover, and temperature.

C. **Remote Sensing Data Acquisition:** The data acquired by satellites is collected in the form of images or digital datasets, including multispectral and hyperspectral imagery, synthetic aperture radar (SAR), and thermal infrared data. These datasets are then transmitted to ground stations for processing and analysis.

D. **Geospatial Information:** Geospatial information, such as the location, elevation, and geographic coordinates of features on the Earth's surface, is critical for remote sensing in archaeology. This information is essential for accurately mapping and analyzing archaeological sites.

## II. Satellite Technologies and Sensors:

A. **Types of Satellites:**

1. **Optical Satellites:** These satellites capture visible and infrared light, providing multispectral or hyperspectral data. Examples include Landsat, Sentinel-2, and MODIS.

2. **Radar Satellites:** Radar satellites, like the European Space Agency's Sentinel-1 and commercial systems such as TerraSAR-X, use microwave wavelengths to penetrate vegetation and clouds, making them ideal for archaeological investigations in tropical regions.

3. **Thermal Infrared Satellites:** These satellites capture thermal emissions from the Earth's surface, helping researchers monitor temperature variations and locate archaeological features based on differences in thermal properties.

B. **Resolution and Spectral Bands:** Satellite sensors vary in spatial resolution, with higher-resolution sensors providing more detailed imagery. Spectral bands, each sensitive to specific wavelengths, offer insights into various surface properties, such as vegetation health, soil moisture, and land cover.

## III. Applications of Satellite-Based Remote Sensing in Archaeology:

A. **Site Detection and Mapping:** Satellite-based remote sensing aids in identifying and mapping archaeological sites, from ancient cities to buried structures and features. It provides an efficient means of surveying large areas and detecting subtle surface anomalies.

B. **Landscape Archaeology:** Researchers employ satellite data to study ancient landscapes, such as terraced fields, irrigation systems, and transportation networks. It helps reveal the organization and evolution of past societies.

C. **Environmental Context:** Satellite imagery is used to assess the environmental context of archaeological sites, including vegetation patterns, topography, and land use. This information offers insights into how ancient societies interacted with their environments.

D. **Cultural Heritage Preservation:** Satellite-based remote sensing assists in the monitoring and preservation of cultural heritage. By tracking site conditions and potential threats, archaeologists and conservationists can prioritize conservation efforts.

E. **Predictive Modeling:** Archaeologists use satellite data to develop predictive models for identifying potential archaeological site locations. These models consider environmental and topographic factors to pinpoint areas likely to contain archaeological remains.

F. **Change Detection:** Satellite imagery captured at different times helps archaeologists monitor changes in archaeological sites. This is crucial for assessing threats like looting, urban development, or environmental degradation.

**IV. Case Studies:**

A. **Angkor Wat, Cambodia:** Satellite imagery has played a pivotal role in revealing the extent of the Angkor Wat temple complex and its surrounding features, including ancient city walls, canals, and reservoirs.

B. **Roman Archaeology in the UK:** Satellite-based remote sensing has identified numerous Roman-era archaeological sites in the UK, including roads, villas, and fortifications.

C. **Nazca Lines, Peru:** The famous Nazca Lines, immense geoglyphs etched into the desert floor, were initially discovered through aerial photography, a precursor to satellite-based remote sensing.

**V. Challenges and Future Directions:**

A. **Data Quality and Resolution:** Improving the spatial and spectral resolution of satellite sensors will enhance the level of detail in archaeological investigations.

B. **Cloud Cover and Weather:** Satellite-based remote sensing can be hampered by cloud cover and adverse weather conditions, limiting data acquisition in some regions.

C. **Data Accessibility:** Ensuring broader access to satellite data for the global archaeological community, especially for developing countries and non-profit research, is an ongoing challenge.

D. **Integration with Ground-Based Techniques:** Integrating satellite data with ground-based methods, such as LiDAR and geophysical surveys, can yield more comprehensive insights into archaeological landscapes.

E. **Advancements in Artificial Intelligence:** The use of machine learning and artificial intelligence in processing and analyzing remote sensing data will improve the efficiency of archaeological investigations.

F. **Community Engagement:** Incorporating local communities and indigenous knowledge into archaeological research and remote sensing projects is vital to ensure cultural sensitivity and preservation of heritage.

Satellite-based remote sensing has undoubtedly transformed the field of archaeology. It offers a non-invasive, cost-effective, and comprehensive means of exploring the Earth's surface, revealing hidden archaeological treasures and contributing to our understanding of ancient civilizations and landscapes. As technology advances and access to data becomes more widespread, the future of satellite-based remote sensing in archaeology is bright, promising more remarkable discoveries and insights into our shared human heritage.

# CHAPTER 5: AERIAL PHOTOGRAPHY AND ARCHAEOLOGICAL MAPPING

Aerial photography and archaeological mapping are fundamental tools in the field of archaeology. This combination of technologies has revolutionized the way archaeologists study and document archaeological sites, enabling them to gain new perspectives, detect hidden features, and create detailed maps of the past. In this comprehensive exploration of aerial photography and archaeological mapping, we will delve into the principles, techniques, applications, and historical significance of these methods in archaeological research.

**I. Fundamental Principles:**

A. **Aerial Photography:** Aerial photography involves capturing images of the Earth's surface from an elevated perspective. These images are usually taken from aircraft, drones, or satellites. Aerial photographs are valuable for archaeological research due to their ability to reveal surface features, such as ancient settlements, fortifications, and crop marks.

B. **Archaeological Mapping:** Archaeological mapping is the process of creating accurate, scaled representations of archaeological sites, landscapes, and features. These maps serve as vital documentation and visualization tools for archaeological investigations, assisting in site preservation and analysis.

**II. Techniques and Technology:**

A. **Aerial Photography:**

1. **Kite and Balloon Photography:** In the early days of aerial photography, kites and balloons were used to

lift cameras and capture images from above. This low-cost method provided a novel perspective for archaeologists.

2. **Aerial Surveys:** Aerial surveys, often conducted using aircraft or drones, involve systematic photography of large areas to detect surface features not easily visible from the ground. These surveys are particularly valuable for identifying crop marks, soil marks, and parch marks that may indicate buried archaeological structures.

3. **Satellite Imagery:** Modern satellite technology has made it possible to capture high-resolution images of archaeological sites and landscapes from space. Satellite imagery provides a global perspective and is widely used for archaeological research.

B. **Archaeological Mapping:**

1. **Total Station Survey:** Total stations are electronic surveying instruments that use electromagnetic distance measurements to record precise positions and elevations of archaeological features. This technology aids in creating accurate site maps.

2. **Geographic Information Systems (GIS):** GIS software enables the integration of spatial and non-spatial data, facilitating the creation of detailed archaeological maps. Archaeologists use GIS to store, analyze, and visualize information related to archaeological sites and landscapes.

3. **LiDAR Technology:** LiDAR (Light Detection and Ranging) technology uses laser pulses to measure the Earth's surface. It is employed to create highly detailed three-dimensional models of terrain, which are valuable for identifying hidden archaeological features and altering the landscape.

## III. Applications of Aerial Photography and Archaeological Mapping:

A. **Site Discovery and Visualization:** Aerial photography and mapping assist in the discovery and documentation of archaeological sites. Aerial imagery reveals the layout of ancient cities, fortifications, and settlements, while mapping provides a visual representation of their features and dimensions.

B. **Landscape Analysis:** These techniques enable archaeologists to understand the broader landscape in which archaeological sites are situated. Researchers can study land use, water management systems, transportation networks, and the relationship between different sites.

C. **Preservation and Conservation:** Aerial photography and mapping are instrumental in preserving archaeological sites and cultural heritage. They assist in monitoring the condition of sites and identifying threats such as looting, erosion, and land development.

D. **Excavation Planning:** Archaeologists use aerial imagery and maps to plan excavations systematically. These tools provide valuable insights into the layout of the site, potentially revealing previously unknown features and guiding excavation strategies.

E. **Environmental Studies:** Aerial photography and mapping are used in environmental archaeology to investigate how ancient societies adapted to and influenced their surroundings. This includes the study of vegetation patterns, land use changes, and soil variations.

## IV. Historical Significance:

A. **Early Use of Aerial Photography:** Aerial photography's contribution to archaeology dates back to the early 20th century when figures like O.G.S. Crawford recognized its potential for archaeological investigations. During World War I and World War II, aerial photographs taken for military purposes inadvertently revealed ancient features and sites.

B. **The Development of Techniques:** Over the years, aerial photography techniques have evolved, transitioning from kite and balloon photography to manned aircraft and, more recently, drones. The development of advanced camera technology and the integration of global positioning systems (GPS) have enhanced the precision and scope of aerial surveys.

C. **The Role of GIS and LiDAR:** The emergence of Geographic Information Systems and LiDAR technology has expanded the capabilities of archaeological mapping. These tools offer more accurate, detailed, and sophisticated ways to visualize archaeological landscapes and uncover hidden features.

**V. Challenges and Future Directions:**

A. **Data Management and Storage:** As data volumes from aerial surveys and mapping increase, efficient data management and storage systems are essential. Archaeologists need to handle and analyze large datasets effectively.

B. **Data Integration:** Integrating data from different sources, including aerial imagery, LiDAR, and ground-based surveys, is a complex but necessary task to create comprehensive archaeological maps.

C. **Technological Advancements:** Continued technological advancements, such as improvements in camera technology and data processing algorithms, will enhance the accuracy and resolution of aerial photography and mapping.

D. **Community Engagement:** Engaging local communities and indigenous knowledge in the archaeological mapping process is essential to respect cultural heritage and ensure preservation.

E. **Machine Learning and Artificial Intelligence:** The use of machine learning and artificial intelligence in data analysis can streamline the process of feature detection in aerial imagery and LiDAR data.

In summary, aerial photography and archaeological mapping are indispensable tools in the archaeologist's toolkit. They provide unique insights into the past, enable the discovery of hidden features, and aid in the preservation and documentation of our cultural heritage. As technology continues to advance and interdisciplinary approaches become more common, the future of aerial photography and archaeological mapping holds promise for uncovering the mysteries of ancient civilizations and landscapes, and contributing to our collective understanding of history.

# CHAPTER 6: LIDAR TECHNOLOGY FOR LANDSCAPE ARCHAEOLOGY

LiDAR (Light Detection and Ranging) technology has emerged as a revolutionary tool for landscape archaeology, significantly enhancing the way researchers study ancient landscapes and archaeological sites. It is a remote sensing technology that uses laser pulses to create highly accurate three-dimensional models of terrain. In this comprehensive exploration of LiDAR technology for landscape archaeology, we will delve into the principles, methods, applications, and the transformative impact it has had on understanding our historical and cultural heritage.

**I. Fundamental Principles:**

A. **LiDAR: The Basics:** LiDAR operates on the principle of emitting laser pulses toward the Earth's surface and measuring the time it takes for the pulse to bounce back. By calculating the distance between the sensor and the target, LiDAR systems generate detailed point clouds that represent the topography and objects on the ground.

B. **Wavelengths and Pulses:** LiDAR can use different wavelengths of light, including visible, near-infrared, and infrared, depending on the specific application. Shorter wavelengths provide higher resolution and accuracy. The laser pulses are emitted in rapid succession, allowing for the creation of millions of data points in a short time.

C. **Data Integration:** LiDAR data is often integrated with other geospatial information, such as GPS (Global Positioning System) and IMU (Inertial Measurement Unit) data, to accurately position and orient the collected points in a geospatial context.

**II. Methods and Data Acquisition:**

A. **Airborne LiDAR:** Airborne LiDAR involves mounting LiDAR sensors on aircraft, such as planes or helicopters. These sensors emit laser pulses and record their return, capturing vast swaths of terrain from the air. Airborne LiDAR is ideal for large-scale landscape archaeology studies.

B. **Terrestrial LiDAR:** Terrestrial LiDAR uses ground-based scanners to capture detailed 3D data of smaller areas. These instruments are often employed in documenting archaeological structures, artifacts, and site features with high precision.

C. **Satellite-Based LiDAR:** Satellite-based LiDAR is a rapidly evolving field that uses spaceborne LiDAR sensors to collect 3D data over large areas. These systems can capture data in a more systematic and repetitive manner, providing valuable information for landscape archaeology.

**III. Applications of LiDAR Technology in Landscape Archaeology:**

A. **Site Discovery and Documentation:** LiDAR is invaluable for discovering previously unknown archaeological features, such as ancient settlements, fortifications, roads, and agricultural systems. The technology provides a non-invasive means of documenting these features in remarkable detail.

B. **Subsurface Mapping:** LiDAR can penetrate vegetation and soil cover to reveal subsurface features, such as buried structures, walls, and roads. This capability is particularly useful in regions with dense vegetation or areas where excavation is challenging.

C. **Understanding Past Landscapes:** LiDAR enables researchers to recreate past landscapes, including topography, water management systems, and land use. It helps archaeologists understand how ancient societies adapted to their environments.

D. **Site Preservation and Conservation:** LiDAR technology assists in monitoring and preserving archaeological sites by assessing site conditions, tracking environmental changes, and identifying potential threats, such as looting, erosion, or urban development.

E. **Predictive Modeling:** LiDAR data can be used to create predictive models for identifying potential archaeological sites based on landscape features, which is particularly helpful in survey planning and cultural resource management.

F. **Archaeological Visualization:** LiDAR data is essential for creating highly detailed 3D visualizations of archaeological sites and landscapes, providing a more comprehensive and immersive experience for researchers and the public.

## IV. Case Studies:

A. **Mayan Cities in Guatemala:** Airborne LiDAR has revealed extensive Mayan cities concealed beneath dense Central American rainforests. The technology has unveiled intricate architectural features, reservoirs, and agricultural terraces, shedding light on the sophisticated nature of Mayan civilization.

B. **Roman Roads in Britain:** LiDAR data has allowed researchers to uncover a network of Roman roads, fortifications, and settlements in the United Kingdom. The technology has played a crucial role in understanding the Roman presence in ancient Britain.

## V. Challenges and Future Directions:

A. **Data Processing and Analysis:** LiDAR data processing can be computationally intensive, requiring specialized software and expertise. Advances in data processing algorithms and machine learning are expected to simplify analysis.

B. **Data Accessibility:** Ensuring broader access to LiDAR data, which is often costly to acquire, will be crucial for researchers, especially those in developing countries and non-profit institutions.

C. **Ethical and Cultural Considerations:** Archaeologists must consider the ethical implications of LiDAR technology, including its impact on local communities and cultural heritage.

Engaging with indigenous knowledge is essential.

D. **Integration with Other Technologies:** Combining LiDAR data with other remote sensing technologies, such as satellite imagery and ground-based surveys, can provide a more comprehensive understanding of archaeological landscapes.

E. **Global Collaboration:** International collaboration is vital for sharing LiDAR data and fostering partnerships in addressing global archaeological challenges.

In summary, LiDAR technology has opened new frontiers in landscape archaeology. It provides a non-invasive means of uncovering hidden archaeological features, reconstructing past landscapes, and preserving cultural heritage. As the technology continues to evolve and data accessibility improves, it holds great promise for uncovering the mysteries of ancient civilizations and landscapes, enhancing our understanding of human history and environmental adaptation.

# CHAPTER 7: GROUND-PENETRATING RADAR IN ARCHAEOLOGICAL INVESTIGATIONS

Ground-Penetrating Radar (GPR) is a non-invasive geophysical technology that has become a fundamental tool in archaeological investigations. GPR allows researchers to explore the subsurface without excavation, providing insights into buried archaeological features, structures, and artifacts. In this comprehensive exploration of GPR in archaeological investigations, we will delve into the principles, methods, applications, case studies, challenges, and the transformative impact it has had on understanding our archaeological past.

## I. Fundamental Principles:

A. **Basic GPR Operation:** GPR operates on the principle of transmitting electromagnetic pulses into the ground and recording the echoes (reflections) of these pulses. The strength and time delay of these reflections are used to create a subsurface image.

B. **Electromagnetic Waves:** GPR uses high-frequency electromagnetic waves, typically in the microwave range. These waves can penetrate the ground and interact with subsurface materials, reflecting back to the surface when encountering boundaries or features with different electrical properties.

C. **Depth and Resolution:** The depth of penetration and resolution of GPR depends on the frequency of the radar system. Higher frequencies provide better resolution but shallower penetration, while lower frequencies can reach greater depths but with reduced resolution.

D. **Data Interpretation:** The data collected by a GPR system are processed to create two-dimensional or three-dimensional images of the subsurface. GPR experts interpret these images to identify archaeological features, such as walls, foundations, burial sites, and artifacts.

## II. Methods and Data Acquisition:

A. **GPR Systems:** GPR systems come in various configurations, including handheld units, cart-mounted systems, and vehicle-mounted arrays. The choice of system depends on the size of the survey area, depth of investigation, and desired resolution.

B. **Survey Design:** Archaeological GPR surveys are carefully planned, considering factors like site size, research objectives, and geological conditions. Grids or transects are established over the survey area, and GPR data are collected at regular intervals.

C. **Data Collection and Processing:** GPR data are collected by moving the radar system over the survey area while recording the signals. The data are then processed to remove noise and create subsurface images, with depth information associated with each feature.

## III. Applications of GPR in Archaeological Investigations:

A. **Site Discovery and Mapping:** GPR is invaluable for detecting buried archaeological sites and features, including walls, foundations, roads, and pits. It aids in mapping the layout and extent of archaeological sites.

B. **Grave Detection:** GPR is widely used in grave detection and cemetery studies. It can locate graves, burial mounds, and crypts, helping in the identification and preservation of human remains.

C. **Artifact Detection:** GPR can identify buried artifacts, such as pottery, metal objects, and tools. This is crucial for understanding the activities and cultures associated with archaeological sites.

D. **Urban Archaeology:** In urban areas, where excavation can be challenging, GPR is essential for assessing the presence of historical structures or buried remains before construction or development.

E. **Forensic Archaeology:** GPR is used in forensic archaeology to locate clandestine burials, helping law enforcement agencies in criminal investigations.

F. **Waterlogged Sites:** GPR is valuable for surveying waterlogged sites, such as sunken ships, submerged settlements, or riverbanks, without excavation or underwater exploration.

**IV. Case Studies:**

A. **The Lost City of the Monkey God, Honduras:** GPR was instrumental in the discovery of a previously unknown archaeological site in Honduras' Mosquitia rainforest. The technology revealed extensive structures hidden beneath the dense jungle canopy, including plazas, pyramids, and ancient roads.

B. **Roman Villa in Italy:** GPR surveys conducted in Italy identified the remains of a Roman villa beneath a vineyard, helping researchers uncover valuable insights into Roman rural life.

**V. Challenges and Future Directions:**

A. **Interpretation and Expertise:** Interpreting GPR data requires expertise, and archaeologists must undergo training to ensure accurate analysis and interpretation of subsurface features.

B. **Site-Specific Conditions:** The effectiveness of GPR can vary depending on site-specific conditions, such as the geology, soil composition, and moisture levels. Researchers must adapt their survey methods accordingly.

C. **Integration with Other Techniques:** Combining GPR with other archaeological and geophysical methods, such as magnetometry and resistivity surveys, can provide a more comprehensive understanding of subsurface features.

D. **Data Analysis Software:** The development of user-friendly data analysis software and machine learning applications can make GPR technology more accessible to archaeologists and streamline the interpretation process.

E. **Ethical Considerations:** In forensic and grave detection applications, ethical considerations and protocols must be followed to ensure the respectful treatment of human remains.

In summary, GPR technology has transformed the field of archaeology, offering a non-invasive means of exploring the subsurface and uncovering hidden archaeological features. As technology continues to advance and the use of GPR becomes more widespread, it holds great promise for uncovering the mysteries of our archaeological past, preserving cultural heritage, and contributing to our collective understanding of history.

# CHAPTER 8: HYPERSPECTRAL IMAGING FOR ARTIFACT DETECTION

Hyperspectral imaging is a cutting-edge technology that has found a wide range of applications in various fields, including remote sensing, agriculture, environmental monitoring, and, significantly, archaeology. In the context of artifact detection, hyperspectral imaging has proven to be a valuable tool for non-invasive exploration, analysis, and preservation of cultural heritage. In this detailed exploration of hyperspectral imaging for artifact detection, we will delve into the fundamental principles, methods, applications, case studies, challenges, and the transformative impact it has had on uncovering and preserving our historical and cultural heritage.

**I. Fundamental Principles:**

A. **What is Hyperspectral Imaging?** Hyperspectral imaging involves the capture of images at hundreds or even thousands of narrow, contiguous spectral bands across the electromagnetic spectrum. These bands span from the visible to the infrared, allowing for highly detailed spectral analysis of the reflected or emitted light from the target.

B. **Spectral Signatures:** Every material has a unique spectral signature, which is a specific pattern of reflectance or absorption at different wavelengths. By analyzing the spectral signature of an object, hyperspectral imaging can distinguish between materials with different compositions and properties.

C. **Spectral Unmixing:** Hyperspectral data can be processed through spectral unmixing algorithms to separate the individual contributions of different materials within a single pixel, allowing for the identification of hidden or mixed materials.

D. **Non-invasive and Non-destructive:** One of the primary advantages of hyperspectral imaging is that it is non-invasive and non-destructive, making it an ideal tool for the examination of delicate artifacts and historical sites.

## II. Methods and Data Acquisition:

A. **Hyperspectral Sensors:** Hyperspectral sensors are designed to capture light in numerous narrow bands across the electromagnetic spectrum. These sensors can be mounted on various platforms, including satellites, aircraft, drones, and ground-based instruments.

B. **Data Processing:** Hyperspectral data is typically represented as a data cube, where each pixel in the image is associated with a spectrum. Data preprocessing and calibration are necessary to convert raw data into usable information.

C. **Spectral Libraries:** Spectral libraries are collections of known spectral signatures from various materials, such as minerals, pigments, and organic compounds. These libraries are essential for comparing and identifying the materials detected in hyperspectral data.

D. **Spectral Unmixing:** Spectral unmixing algorithms are applied to hyperspectral data to estimate the proportion of different materials contributing to each pixel in the image. This process helps identify materials that may be hidden within an artifact or structure.

## III. Applications of Hyperspectral Imaging in Artifact Detection:

A. **Identification of Pigments:** Hyperspectral imaging is used to identify and characterize pigments used in artworks and murals. By analyzing the reflectance spectra, conservators and art historians can gain insights into the painting techniques and identify hidden layers or alterations.

B. **Ancient Manuscript Analysis:** In the study of ancient

manuscripts, hyperspectral imaging is applied to reveal faded or erased texts that are no longer visible to the naked eye. This has uncovered lost writings and insights into the history of ancient documents.

C. **Archaeological Prospection:** Hyperspectral imaging aids in the detection of archaeological features hidden beneath the ground, such as buried walls, foundations, and ancient roads. It is also instrumental in identifying crop marks and soil anomalies that may indicate subsurface structures.

D. **Artifact Provenance Studies:** Hyperspectral imaging can be employed to determine the geographic origin of artifacts by analyzing the chemical composition of the materials used in their construction.

E. **Artwork Conservation:** In the conservation of cultural heritage, hyperspectral imaging helps assess the condition of artifacts, frescoes, and paintings, aiding conservators in planning preservation and restoration efforts.

**IV. Case Studies:**

A. **Villa of the Papyri, Herculaneum:** Hyperspectral imaging was used to read the carbonized papyrus scrolls recovered from the Villa of the Papyri, a Roman villa buried by the eruption of Mount Vesuvius. This technology has helped uncover and decipher ancient texts that were thought to be lost.

B. **Machu Picchu, Peru:** Hyperspectral imaging was applied to analyze the vegetation surrounding Machu Picchu. This revealed the Inca agricultural terraces and their irrigation system, offering insights into the sustainable land use practices of the ancient civilization.

**V. Challenges and Future Directions:**

A. **Data Processing and Storage:** Hyperspectral data processing can be computationally intensive, requiring robust data management and storage solutions.

B. **Equipment Accessibility:** Acquiring hyperspectral imaging equipment and expertise can be challenging for many archaeological teams, particularly those with limited resources.

C. **Standardization and Integration:** Developing standards for hyperspectral data acquisition and integration with other archaeological techniques is essential for expanding its applications and accessibility.

D. **Ethical Considerations:** In the conservation of cultural heritage, ethical considerations and cultural sensitivities must be addressed when using hyperspectral imaging, particularly when dealing with sacred or culturally significant artifacts.

E. **Advancements in Machine Learning:** The integration of machine learning and artificial intelligence in hyperspectral data analysis holds potential for automating material identification and object recognition.

In summary, hyperspectral imaging has become a transformative technology in the field of artifact detection and archaeological investigations. It enables the non-invasive exploration, analysis, and preservation of cultural heritage, contributing to a deeper understanding of our historical past. As technology continues to advance and accessibility to hyperspectral imaging tools improves, it promises to unveil more hidden treasures and expand our knowledge of ancient civilizations and their cultural expressions.

# CHAPTER 9: INFRARED THERMOGRAPHY IN ARCHAEOLOGICAL PROSPECTION

Infrared thermography, also known as thermal imaging or thermographic imaging, is an advanced non-invasive technology that has been increasingly employed in archaeological prospection. It offers a unique way to explore and uncover hidden archaeological features, assess the structural condition of historical buildings, and study landscapes. In this comprehensive exploration of infrared thermography in archaeological prospection, we will delve into the fundamental principles, methods, applications, case studies, challenges, and the transformative impact it has had on understanding our archaeological heritage.

## I. Fundamental Principles:

A. **Thermal Imaging Basics:** Infrared thermography involves capturing and visualizing the temperature distribution of an object or a scene by detecting the infrared radiation it emits. Every object with a temperature above absolute zero emits infrared radiation in the form of heat. Thermal cameras capture this radiation and convert it into a thermal image, which is then superimposed on a regular visual image or displayed separately in false colors.

B. **Temperature Variations:** Archaeological materials and structures have different thermal properties and heat capacities than the surrounding soil or environment. This results in temperature variations that can be detected and analyzed using infrared thermography.

C. **Time-Dependent Analysis:** Infrared thermography often involves time-dependent analysis. The study area is surveyed at various times, allowing the researcher to identify thermal anomalies and patterns that might indicate the presence of buried features or structures.

## II. Methods and Data Acquisition:

A. **Instruments and Sensors:** Infrared thermography relies on specialized thermal cameras or sensors that can detect and record infrared radiation. These instruments vary in terms of resolution, sensitivity, and the range of wavelengths they can capture.

B. **Data Collection:** Archaeological thermographic surveys involve collecting thermal data in various ways, such as handheld surveys, aerial or drone-based imaging, and even ground-based systems for large-scale landscape prospection.

C. **Data Processing and Analysis:** The raw thermal data is processed to create thermal images. Software tools are used to analyze these images, highlighting temperature variations and potential archaeological features. These analyses often involve the detection of thermal anomalies that might signify buried structures, subsurface walls, or disturbed areas.

## III. Applications of Infrared Thermography in Archaeological Prospection:

A. **Site Discovery and Mapping:** Infrared thermography can reveal previously unknown archaeological features, such as buried walls, foundations, and ditches. It helps archaeologists map the layout and extent of archaeological sites and structures.

B. **Waterlogged Site Investigations:** Thermal imaging is particularly useful for examining waterlogged sites and submerged structures. It can identify subsurface features that might be hidden underwater.

C. **Conservation and Preservation:** Infrared thermography plays a crucial role in assessing the structural condition of historical buildings, monuments, and artworks. It aids in conservation efforts by identifying areas of potential decay or structural instability.

D. **Landscape Studies:** In landscape archaeology, thermal imaging is used to study land use patterns, agricultural practices, and the presence of hidden features such as ancient roads, terraces, and field boundaries.

E. **Environmental Archaeology:** By assessing temperature variations, thermography can help archaeologists understand how ancient societies adapted to their environments, such as through land use and agricultural practices.

**IV. Case Studies:**

A. **Catalhoyuk, Turkey:** Infrared thermography has been employed to explore the ancient settlement of Catalhoyuk, revealing the buried remains of buildings and wall structures. This technology has provided valuable insights into the architectural layout of the site.

B. **Pompeii, Italy:** Thermal imaging has been used in Pompeii to detect and map the buried ruins of structures and roads, which were concealed by volcanic ash and lava during the eruption of Mount Vesuvius in 79 AD.

**V. Challenges and Future Directions:**

A. **Data Interpretation:** Interpreting thermal data can be challenging, as temperature variations can result from various factors, including natural processes and modern disturbances.

B. **Data Resolution:** The level of detail and resolution in thermal images can vary depending on the equipment used. Advancements in thermal imaging technology are expected to provide higher-resolution images.

C. **Data Synchronization:** Integrating thermal data with other archaeological information, such as geospatial data and historical records, is essential for comprehensive archaeological investigations.

D. **Interdisciplinary Collaboration:** Archaeologists often collaborate with experts in remote sensing, geophysics, and building conservation to make the most of thermal imaging in their research.

E. **Global Accessibility:** Enhancing the accessibility of thermal imaging technology to archaeologists in developing countries and non-profit research organizations is crucial for expanding its applications.

In summary, infrared thermography has become an invaluable tool in archaeological prospection, allowing researchers to uncover hidden archaeological features, assess the condition of historical structures, and study landscapes in a non-invasive manner. As technology continues to advance and the interdisciplinary use of thermography becomes more common, it promises to shed more light on our archaeological heritage, revealing hidden treasures and expanding our understanding of ancient civilizations and their interactions with their environments.

# CHAPTER 10: 3D MODELING AND ARCHAEOLOGICAL VISUALIZATION

3D modeling and archaeological visualization are advanced techniques that have transformed the field of archaeology. These methods provide powerful tools for the study, analysis, and communication of archaeological sites, artifacts, and landscapes. In this comprehensive exploration of 3D modeling and archaeological visualization, we will delve into the fundamental principles, methods, applications, case studies, challenges, and the transformative impact they have had on our understanding of the past.

## I. Fundamental Principles:

A. **What is 3D Modeling?** 3D modeling is the process of creating a digital representation of a three-dimensional object or space. In archaeology, this can include archaeological artifacts, structures, and entire landscapes.

B. **3D Visualization:** 3D visualization refers to the presentation and exploration of 3D models. It can be used for analysis, documentation, interpretation, and communication of archaeological data.

C. **Data Sources:** Data for 3D modeling in archaeology can come from a variety of sources, including laser scanning (LiDAR), photogrammetry, drone imagery, ground-based surveys, and more.

D. **Geospatial Data Integration:** 3D models are often integrated with geospatial data to place archaeological features within a specific geographical context.

## II. Methods and Data Acquisition:

A. **Photogrammetry:** Photogrammetry involves taking numerous photographs of an object or site from various angles and then processing these images to create a 3D model. It is widely used in archaeology for artifact documentation and site recording.

B. **Laser Scanning (LiDAR):** LiDAR technology uses laser pulses to measure distances, making it highly accurate for capturing 3D data. Archaeologists use LiDAR for landscape modeling and the identification of archaeological features.

C. **Structure from Motion (SfM):** Structure from Motion is a photogrammetric technique that involves generating 3D models from 2D image sequences. It is especially useful for site documentation and artifact reconstruction.

D. **Drones and UAVs:** Unmanned aerial vehicles (UAVs) equipped with cameras and LiDAR sensors have become essential for capturing aerial imagery and creating 3D models of large archaeological sites and landscapes.

E. **Ground-Penetrating Radar (GPR):** GPR can be used to gather subsurface data that can be incorporated into 3D models to visualize buried archaeological features.

**III. Applications of 3D Modeling and Archaeological Visualization:**

A. **Site Reconstruction:** 3D models enable archaeologists to recreate ancient structures and settlements, providing a visual representation of how these sites might have looked in the past.

B. **Artifact Analysis:** Archaeologists use 3D models to examine and analyze artifacts in detail, making it easier to study inscriptions, carvings, and the manufacturing techniques of ancient objects.

C. **Landscape Visualization:** 3D models of landscapes help researchers study ancient topography, land use patterns, and how human societies adapted to their environments.

D. **Virtual Reality (VR) and Augmented Reality (AR):**

Archaeological 3D models can be used to create immersive experiences in virtual reality or augmented reality, allowing users to explore ancient sites or artifacts in a more interactive way.

E. **Public Outreach and Education:** 3D models are used to engage the public and make archaeology more accessible. Virtual tours, interactive exhibits, and 3D-printed artifacts can be part of museum displays and educational resources.

## IV. Case Studies:

A. **Pompeii, Italy:** Archaeologists have used 3D modeling and visualization to recreate the ancient city of Pompeii, showcasing its architecture and daily life before the catastrophic eruption of Mount Vesuvius in 79 AD.

B. **Stonehenge, United Kingdom:** LiDAR data and 3D modeling have provided new insights into the landscape and the positioning of stones at Stonehenge, shedding light on its construction and use.

## V. Challenges and Future Directions:

A. **Data Integration and Standardization:** Integrating data from various sources and ensuring standardized data formats are crucial for accurate 3D modeling.

B. **Data Processing and Storage:** Managing and processing large datasets for 3D modeling can be challenging, necessitating advanced computing resources.

C. **Accessibility and Training:** Making 3D modeling techniques accessible to a broader range of archaeologists and institutions requires training and resource sharing.

D. **Ethical Considerations:** Archaeologists must consider ethical issues when using 3D modeling, such as the digital reproduction of cultural heritage and the protection of sensitive archaeological data.

E. **Advancements in Visualization Technologies:** As technology continues to evolve, the use of 3D modeling in archaeology is expected to become more integrated with other visualization technologies like virtual reality and augmented reality.

In summary, 3D modeling and archaeological visualization have revolutionized the field of archaeology, offering powerful tools for the analysis and communication of archaeological data. They provide new ways to explore and understand the past, making it more accessible to both researchers and the public. As technology continues to advance, the future of 3D modeling in archaeology promises to uncover more hidden treasures, deepen our understanding of ancient civilizations, and expand the possibilities for studying our shared history.

# CHAPTER 11: MULTISPECTRAL REMOTE SENSING IN VEGETATION ANALYSIS

Multispectral remote sensing is a powerful and versatile technology that has significantly advanced the field of vegetation analysis. It involves the collection of data from multiple spectral bands across the electromagnetic spectrum, allowing researchers to study vegetation health, composition, distribution, and ecological interactions with remarkable precision. In this comprehensive exploration of multispectral remote sensing in vegetation analysis, we will delve into the fundamental principles, methods, applications, case studies, challenges, and the transformative impact it has had on our understanding of ecosystems, land management, and environmental conservation.

## I. Fundamental Principles:

A. **What is Multispectral Remote Sensing?** Multispectral remote sensing involves capturing information from various spectral bands beyond the visible light spectrum, including infrared and ultraviolet wavelengths. Each spectral band conveys unique information about the Earth's surface, including vegetation.

B. **Spectral Signatures:** Different types of vegetation exhibit distinctive spectral signatures. These signatures are patterns of reflectance and absorption of light across the spectral bands, allowing researchers to identify and study specific plant species or assess their health.

C. **Radiation Interactions:** Plants interact with electromagnetic radiation through processes like absorption, reflection, and transmission. Chlorophyll in leaves, for instance, strongly absorbs red and blue light while reflecting green light. These interactions serve as the basis for multispectral vegetation analysis.

D. **Vegetation Indices:** Researchers often use vegetation indices, such as the Normalized Difference Vegetation Index (NDVI) or the Enhanced Vegetation Index (EVI), to quantify vegetation properties like greenness, photosynthetic activity, and leaf area.

## II. Methods and Data Acquisition:

A. **Remote Sensing Platforms:** Multispectral data can be collected from various platforms, including satellites, aircraft, drones, and ground-based sensors. Satellite-based sensors like MODIS, Landsat, and Sentinel missions are essential for large-scale vegetation monitoring.

B. **Sensors and Instruments:** Multispectral sensors can be passive, relying on sunlight to capture data, or active, using emitted radiation. Hyperspectral sensors, which capture a greater number of narrow bands, provide even more detailed spectral information.

C. **Spectral Resolution:** Spectral resolution refers to the number and width of spectral bands in the sensor. Higher spectral resolution provides more detailed information but may come at the cost of spatial resolution.

D. **Data Processing and Analysis:** Multispectral data are processed to create images or maps that display vegetation properties. Image analysis techniques, such as supervised or unsupervised classification, are used to identify different vegetation types and analyze their characteristics.

## III. Applications of Multispectral Remote Sensing in Vegetation Analysis:

A. **Vegetation Health Monitoring:** Multispectral data can be used to assess the health of vegetation, including detecting signs of stress, disease, or nutrient deficiencies. Changes in NDVI values over time can indicate alterations in plant condition.

B. **Biodiversity Assessment:** Researchers use multispectral data to estimate biodiversity by mapping and monitoring the distribution of different plant species and ecosystems.

C. **Land Use and Land Cover Change:** Multispectral remote sensing helps monitor changes in land use and land cover, such as deforestation, urban expansion, and agricultural practices, which have a significant impact on vegetation.

D. **Forest Management:** Forestry professionals rely on multispectral data to evaluate the volume, age, and species composition of forests. This information is crucial for sustainable forest management.

E. **Agriculture:** Multispectral data are extensively used in precision agriculture to optimize crop yield, assess soil fertility, and manage irrigation.

F. **Wetland Conservation:** Wetland ecosystems are crucial for biodiversity and carbon storage. Multispectral data aid in the identification and monitoring of wetland areas.

## IV. Case Studies:

A. **Amazon Rainforest Monitoring:** Satellite-based multispectral remote sensing has been pivotal in monitoring deforestation in the Amazon rainforest. It helps detect illegal logging activities and assess the impacts of land use change on this vital ecosystem.

B. **Great Barrier Reef, Australia:** Multispectral data have been used to study the health of coral reefs, including assessing coral bleaching events caused by rising sea temperatures. This information is crucial for the conservation of these vulnerable ecosystems.

## V. Challenges and Future Directions:

A. **Data Quality and Availability:** Access to high-quality multispectral data can be limited, and cloud cover or atmospheric interference can affect data quality.

B. **Data Processing Complexity:** Processing multispectral data and performing accurate image analysis require specialized software and expertise.

C. **Data Integration:** Integrating multispectral data with other geospatial information, such as terrain data and climate records, is crucial for comprehensive vegetation analysis.

D. **Temporal Resolution:** Temporal resolution refers to how often data are acquired. Frequent revisits by satellites and the development of constellations aim to improve temporal resolution.

E. **Advancements in Sensors:** Ongoing technological advancements in sensors are expected to yield more capable multispectral instruments with improved spatial and spectral resolution.

In summary, multispectral remote sensing has revolutionized vegetation analysis, providing essential insights into the health, distribution, and dynamics of plant life on Earth. It plays a central role in environmental monitoring, conservation efforts, and land management practices. As technology continues to advance, the future of multispectral remote sensing promises even greater contributions to our understanding of ecosystems and the mitigation of environmental challenges. It will remain a vital tool in the study and protection of our planet's diverse vegetation.

# CHAPTER 12: GEOSPATIAL ANALYSIS IN ARCHAEOLOGICAL RESEARCH

Geospatial analysis is a powerful approach that has significantly enriched archaeological research and transformed the field. It involves the use of geographic information systems (GIS), remote sensing, and other spatial technologies to study and understand archaeological sites, landscapes, and artifacts. In this comprehensive exploration of geospatial analysis in archaeological research, we will delve into the fundamental principles, methods, applications, case studies, challenges, and the transformative impact it has had on our understanding of past civilizations and human history.

**I. Fundamental Principles:**

A. **What is Geospatial Analysis?** Geospatial analysis is the application of spatial and geographic techniques to archaeological data. It allows researchers to integrate, analyze, and visualize various types of spatial information, including maps, satellite imagery, and topographic data.

B. **Spatial Data:** Archaeological research often involves the collection of spatial data, including the precise location of archaeological features, artifacts, and the topography of excavation sites. Geospatial analysis enables the management and analysis of these datasets.

C. **Geographic Information Systems (GIS):** GIS is a core tool in geospatial analysis. It is a computer-based system for capturing, storing, managing, analyzing, and presenting geospatial data. Archaeologists use GIS to map and analyze the distribution of archaeological sites, features, and artifacts.

D. **Remote Sensing:** Remote sensing technologies, such as

aerial photography, LiDAR, and multispectral imagery, provide valuable data for geospatial analysis in archaeology. These technologies allow researchers to capture information about the Earth's surface from a distance.

**II. Methods and Data Acquisition:**

A. **Geospatial Data Sources:** Archaeologists acquire geospatial data from various sources, including ground surveys, satellite and aerial imagery, historic maps, LiDAR, and GPS data. Combining these sources provides a more comprehensive understanding of archaeological contexts.

B. **GPS Technology:** Global Positioning System (GPS) technology is used to record the precise location of archaeological features, enabling the creation of accurate maps and spatial databases.

C. **Remote Sensing Techniques:** LiDAR technology is used for capturing high-resolution topographic data. Aerial photography and multispectral imagery aid in site detection, mapping, and landscape analysis.

D. **Data Processing and Analysis:** Data collected through various means are processed and analyzed using GIS software. Spatial queries, spatial statistics, and modeling are applied to answer specific research questions.

**III. Applications of Geospatial Analysis in Archaeological Research:**

A. **Site Detection and Mapping:** Geospatial analysis aids in the identification, mapping, and monitoring of archaeological sites, structures, and features. It has led to the discovery of previously unknown settlements and landscapes.

B. **Landscape Archaeology:** Researchers use geospatial analysis to study how ancient civilizations interacted with their environments. This includes examining land use patterns, agricultural practices, and the impact of climate change on landscapes.

C. **Excavation Planning:** GIS is essential for planning

archaeological excavations. It helps researchers select excavation sites, prioritize areas of interest, and manage excavation records.

D. **Artifact Analysis:** Geospatial analysis enables researchers to record the precise locations of artifacts within a site, allowing for the spatial analysis of artifact distribution and patterns.

E. **Heritage Preservation:** GIS is used for heritage management, aiding in the preservation and protection of archaeological sites and cultural heritage.

F. **Cultural Resource Management:** Geospatial analysis is essential in cultural resource management, helping assess the impact of development projects on archaeological sites and ensuring their protection.

**IV. Case Studies:**

A. **Angkor, Cambodia:** Geospatial analysis has been used to uncover the extent and complexity of the Angkor civilization. LiDAR data revealed hidden temples, canals, and infrastructure in the Cambodian jungle.

B. **Pompeii, Italy:** GIS and remote sensing technologies have played a crucial role in the documentation and management of the ancient city of Pompeii and the surrounding landscape.

**V. Challenges and Future Directions:**

A. **Data Integration:** Integrating diverse datasets and formats from different sources can be challenging, and standardization is essential.

B. **Accessibility and Training:** Access to geospatial tools and expertise can be limited for some archaeological researchers and institutions, highlighting the need for training and resources.

C. **Ethical Considerations:** Researchers must address ethical issues, including the protection of cultural heritage and respecting the rights and concerns of local communities.

D. **Interdisciplinary Collaboration:** Collaboration between archaeologists, geospatial experts, and other specialists is essential for advancing geospatial analysis in archaeology.

E. **Advancements in Technology:** Continual advancements in remote sensing, LiDAR, and GIS technologies will open new possibilities for archaeological research.

In summary, geospatial analysis has revolutionized archaeological research, providing invaluable tools for site detection, mapping, landscape analysis, and cultural resource management. It has uncovered hidden treasures, deepened our understanding of past civilizations, and contributed to the preservation of cultural heritage. As technology continues to advance and interdisciplinary collaborations expand, the future of geospatial analysis in archaeology promises to unveil more of our shared human history and the rich tapestry of archaeological discoveries.

# CHAPTER 13: SITE SELECTION AND PREDICTIVE MODELING WITH GIS

Site selection and predictive modeling with Geographic Information Systems (GIS) is a vital component of various fields, including archaeology, urban planning, environmental management, and more. GIS provides the tools and techniques to make informed decisions about where to locate new sites, facilities, or developments, taking into account a multitude of spatial and non-spatial factors. In this comprehensive exploration of site selection and predictive modeling with GIS, we will delve into the fundamental principles, methods, applications, case studies, challenges, and the transformative impact it has had on planning, development, and conservation efforts.

## I. Fundamental Principles:

A. **What is Site Selection and Predictive Modeling?** Site selection involves the process of choosing the most suitable location for a particular project, development, or research based on a set of predefined criteria. Predictive modeling uses historical and spatial data to predict future trends, conditions, or outcomes. In combination, they help make informed decisions.

B. **Spatial and Non-Spatial Data:** Site selection and predictive modeling in GIS rely on both spatial and non-spatial data. Spatial data includes geographic information like location, topography, and proximity to resources. Non-spatial data encompasses factors such as economic conditions, demographics, and environmental regulations.

C. **Criteria and Weights:** Decision-makers establish criteria for site selection, assigning weights to each criterion to reflect its relative importance. GIS enables the quantification and analysis of these criteria.

D. **Spatial Analysis:** GIS facilitates spatial analysis by integrating different data layers, performing geoprocessing tasks, and creating spatial models that assess the suitability of sites based on predefined criteria.

## II. Methods and Data Acquisition:

A. **Geospatial Data Sources:** GIS uses a wide range of geospatial data sources, including satellite imagery, aerial photography, LiDAR data, land use maps, and remotely sensed data to inform site selection and predictive modeling.

B. **Field Surveys:** Field surveys and data collection play a significant role in confirming the suitability of a site. This may include ground-truthing to validate and refine GIS-based predictions.

C. **Data Preprocessing:** Data preprocessing involves data cleaning, integration, and transformation to prepare the information for use in GIS analysis. This includes georeferencing and data conversion.

D. **Modeling Techniques:** Various modeling techniques are employed in GIS, including suitability modeling, suitability index, weighted overlay, and multi-criteria decision analysis (MCDA) models. These techniques help assess site suitability based on spatial criteria.

## III. Applications of Site Selection and Predictive Modeling with GIS:

A. **Urban Planning:** GIS is used in urban planning to select suitable locations for infrastructure development, zoning decisions, and land use planning. It aids in optimizing transportation networks, public facilities, and green spaces.

B. **Environmental Conservation:** Site selection is vital in the establishment of conservation areas, wildlife reserves, and protected zones. GIS helps identify habitats, corridors, and regions with high biodiversity.

C. **Business Site Selection:** GIS is employed by businesses for location-based decisions, including where to open new retail outlets, distribution centers, or manufacturing plants.

D. **Agriculture and Farming:** In agriculture, GIS helps farmers decide where to plant crops, where to apply fertilizers, and how to manage irrigation efficiently.

E. **Archaeological Site Discovery:** Archaeologists use predictive modeling to locate potential archaeological sites based on terrain, historical records, and other spatial data.

**IV. Case Studies:**

A. **Wind Farm Site Selection:** In the development of wind farms, GIS is used to identify locations with optimal wind conditions, accessibility, and minimal environmental impact.

B. **Conservation of Endangered Species:** GIS is integral to identifying critical habitats for endangered species, helping conservation efforts target areas that are most vital for their survival.

**V. Challenges and Future Directions:**

A. **Data Quality:** Ensuring data quality, accuracy, and consistency is a persistent challenge in GIS, as inaccurate or incomplete data can lead to suboptimal decisions.

B. **Model Complexity:** As GIS models become more complex, they require robust computational resources and skilled analysts.

C. **Interdisciplinary Collaboration:** Interdisciplinary collaboration between GIS experts, domain specialists, and stakeholders is essential to produce effective site selection and predictive models.

D. **Privacy and Ethics:** The use of GIS in location-based decision-making raises ethical concerns about privacy and the potential misuse of spatial data.

E. **Advancements in Technology:** The future of site selection and predictive modeling in GIS lies in technological advancements, including improved data sources, cloud-based GIS, and the integration of real-time data streams.

In summary, site selection and predictive modeling with GIS have become indispensable tools in decision-making across various fields. They enable informed choices about where to locate new developments, how to protect the environment, and where to allocate resources. As GIS technology continues to advance and interdisciplinary collaboration expands, it promises to play an even more prominent role in enhancing spatial decision-making and shaping our world in a sustainable and efficient manner.

# CHAPTER 14: DRONES AND UNMANNED AERIAL VEHICLES IN ARCHAEOLOGY

Drones and Unmanned Aerial Vehicles (UAVs) have rapidly become essential tools in the field of archaeology. These aerial platforms have transformed archaeological research by providing new ways to survey, document, and analyze archaeological sites, landscapes, and artifacts. In this comprehensive exploration of drones and UAVs in archaeology, we will delve into the fundamental principles, methods, applications, case studies, challenges, and the transformative impact they have had on our understanding of the past.

**I. Fundamental Principles:**

A. **What are Drones and UAVs?** Drones, also known as Unmanned Aerial Vehicles (UAVs) or Unmanned Aircraft Systems (UAS), are aerial platforms without a human pilot on board. They are typically controlled remotely and can be equipped with various sensors and cameras for data collection.

B. **Aerial Survey and Documentation:** Drones provide a bird's-eye view of archaeological sites and landscapes. They are used to capture high-resolution aerial imagery and generate 3D models of the terrain.

C. **Remote Sensing Sensors:** Drones can carry a range of remote sensing sensors, such as visible light cameras, multispectral cameras, LiDAR (Light Detection and Ranging), and thermal cameras. These sensors capture data that can reveal archaeological features not easily visible from the ground.

D. **Geospatial Data Integration:** Drones are often used in conjunction with Geographic Information Systems (GIS) to georeference and analyze the spatial data collected. This integration helps archaeologists create accurate maps and models.

**II. Methods and Data Acquisition:**

A. **Types of Drones:** Different types of drones are used in archaeology, ranging from small consumer-grade quadcopters to fixed-wing UAVs. The choice of drone depends on the specific archaeological objectives and the required flight endurance.

B. **Data Acquisition:** Drones capture data through aerial photography, photogrammetry, LiDAR, and other remote sensing techniques. Aerial images are taken at different angles, which can be processed to generate 3D models.

C. **Real-time Monitoring:** Some drones offer real-time monitoring capabilities, allowing archaeologists to assess data quality and adjust flight plans while in the field.

D. **Post-Processing:** Data collected by drones are processed using specialized software to create orthomosaics, digital elevation models, and 3D reconstructions.

**III. Applications of Drones and UAVs in Archaeology:**

A. **Site Discovery and Mapping:** Drones are used to identify and map archaeological sites, including features like ancient roads, fortifications, and burial mounds.

B. **Aerial Photography and Videography:** Drones capture stunning aerial photographs and videos of archaeological sites, which are useful for documentation, site promotion, and educational purposes.

C. **3D Modeling:** Drones are employed to generate high-resolution 3D models of archaeological features, structures, and landscapes, aiding in detailed analysis and visualization.

D. **LiDAR Scanning:** LiDAR-equipped drones are particularly useful for forested areas, as they can penetrate vegetation to reveal hidden archaeological features, including ancient settlements and earthworks.

E. **Monitoring and Conservation:** Drones assist in monitoring the condition of archaeological sites and heritage structures. They are also used to create digital archives of at-risk sites.

F. **Agricultural Archaeology:** Drones are applied in the study of agricultural practices of ancient civilizations, including the mapping of terraced fields and irrigation systems.

**IV. Case Studies:**

A. **Caracol, Belize:** Drones were used to map the ancient Maya city of Caracol, revealing extensive urban infrastructure and agricultural terraces hidden beneath the forest canopy.

B. **Stonehenge, United Kingdom:** Drones have been employed to create 3D models and assess the condition of the Stonehenge monument, aiding in its conservation.

**V. Challenges and Future Directions:**

A. **Regulation and Ethics:** Drones are subject to regulations that vary by country, and ethical considerations, including privacy concerns, must be addressed.

B. **Data Processing:** Processing and managing the large amounts of data collected by drones can be complex and resource-intensive.

C. **Integration with Other Technologies:** Drones are increasingly being used in conjunction with other remote sensing technologies, such as ground-penetrating radar and multispectral imaging.

D. **Accessibility and Training:** Access to drones and training in their operation and data processing can be limiting factors for many archaeological teams.

E. **Future Advancements:** Advancements in drone technology are expected to enhance their capabilities, including longer flight times, more sophisticated sensors, and improved automation for data collection and processing.

In summary, drones and UAVs have revolutionized

archaeological research by providing an aerial perspective that was previously unattainable or cost-prohibitive. They have facilitated site discovery, mapping, documentation, and analysis of archaeological features and landscapes. As technology continues to advance and the use of drones becomes more accessible, their role in uncovering and preserving our shared human heritage is expected to expand, offering new insights into the past and aiding in the protection of archaeological sites for future generations.

# CHAPTER 15: TERRESTRIAL LASER SCANNING IN SITE DOCUMENTATION

Terrestrial Laser Scanning (TLS), also known as ground-based LiDAR (Light Detection and Ranging), is a cutting-edge technology that has revolutionized site documentation in various fields, including archaeology, architecture, engineering, and cultural heritage preservation. It offers a highly precise and efficient means of capturing detailed 3D representations of objects, structures, and landscapes. In this comprehensive exploration of terrestrial laser scanning in site documentation, we will delve into the fundamental principles, methods, applications, case studies, challenges, and the transformative impact it has had on our ability to record and understand the physical world.

**I. Fundamental Principles:**

A. **What is Terrestrial Laser Scanning?** Terrestrial Laser Scanning is a remote sensing technique that uses laser pulses to measure distances and capture detailed 3D data of objects or environments. It provides a precise representation of the shape and location of surfaces.

B. **Laser Scanning Process:** TLS instruments emit laser beams that reflect off the surfaces they encounter. The instrument measures the time it takes for the laser beam to return, calculating the distance to the target point. By scanning many points rapidly, it creates a "point cloud" of millions of 3D coordinates.

C. **Data Accuracy:** TLS is highly accurate, capable of capturing objects or features with sub-millimeter precision. The accuracy of the data is crucial for many applications, including archaeology and engineering.

D. **Rapid Data Collection:** TLS can capture a vast amount of data in a relatively short time, making it efficient for site documentation, even in complex and cluttered environments.

**II. Methods and Data Acquisition:**

A. **TLS Instruments:** TLS instruments vary in size and complexity, from small, portable scanners to larger systems with multiple laser emitters and high-resolution cameras. The choice of instrument depends on the specific documentation needs.

B. **Data Collection Workflow:** Terrestrial Laser Scanning involves setting up the scanner at different locations to capture a site from multiple angles. This results in a more comprehensive point cloud that includes all surfaces, including those hidden from a single scan.

C. **Integration with Other Technologies:** TLS data can be integrated with other technologies such as digital photography, GPS, and total station measurements to enhance the documentation process.

D. **Data Registration:** After capturing data from various scanner positions, the scans must be accurately registered together to create a complete and coherent 3D model of the site or object.

**III. Applications of Terrestrial Laser Scanning in Site Documentation:**

A. **Archaeology:** TLS is used to document archaeological sites, artifacts, and excavations. It aids in recording stratigraphy, site layouts, and architectural features with a high level of precision.

B. **Cultural Heritage Preservation:** TLS is invaluable for documenting historical buildings, sculptures, and cultural heritage sites. It assists in conservation and restoration efforts by creating accurate 3D models for analysis.

C. **Engineering and Construction:** Engineers and construction professionals use TLS for site documentation and quality control. It helps monitor structural deformations and document construction progress.

D. **Forensics:** In forensic investigations, TLS can accurately capture crime scenes, accident sites, and evidence, assisting in the reconstruction of events.

E. **Architecture and Design:** Architects and designers use TLS to create as-built documentation of existing structures and environments, which is essential for renovation and retrofit projects.

F. **Environmental Monitoring:** TLS is used to monitor natural landscapes, including coastal erosion, rockfall hazards, and glacial retreat.

**IV. Case Studies:**

A. **Laser Scanning of Machu Picchu, Peru:** TLS was used to document and analyze the architecture and landscape of Machu Picchu, revealing structural details and geological characteristics that were previously unknown.

B. **Documentation of the Notre-Dame Cathedral, Paris:** After the 2019 fire at the Notre-Dame Cathedral, TLS was employed to document the extent of the damage and aid in the restoration efforts.

**V. Challenges and Future Directions:**

A. **Data Management:** The large volume of data generated by TLS requires effective data management and storage solutions.

B. **Integration with BIM:** The integration of TLS data with Building Information Modeling (BIM) is becoming increasingly important in the construction and architectural industries.

C. **Cost and Accessibility:** Although the cost of TLS instruments has decreased over the years, access to the technology and expertise remains a challenge for many organizations.

D. **Automation and Artificial Intelligence:** Advancements in automation and artificial intelligence are expected to streamline the data processing and interpretation of TLS data.

E. **Environmental Considerations:** TLS instruments have environmental impacts, including energy consumption. Energy-efficient scanning methods and sustainable practices are being explored.

In summary, terrestrial laser scanning has revolutionized site documentation by providing a highly accurate, efficient, and non-destructive means of capturing 3D representations of objects, structures, and landscapes. It has had a transformative impact on archaeological research, architectural preservation, engineering, and many other fields. As technology continues to advance and access to TLS becomes more widespread, it promises to further revolutionize the way we document and understand the physical world around us.

# CHAPTER 16: REMOTE SENSING AND UNDERWATER ARCHAEOLOGY

Remote sensing, a powerful technology widely used in various fields, plays a pivotal role in underwater archaeology. It provides a means to explore and study submerged cultural heritage, shipwrecks, submerged settlements, and archaeological sites beneath the world's oceans, seas, and lakes. In this extensive exploration of remote sensing in underwater archaeology, we will delve into the fundamental principles, methods, applications, case studies, challenges, and the transformative impact it has had on our understanding of submerged history.

## I. Fundamental Principles:

A. **What is Remote Sensing in Underwater Archaeology?** Remote sensing in underwater archaeology involves the use of technology to collect data about submerged archaeological sites without direct physical contact. It encompasses a range of methods, including sonar, magnetometry, photogrammetry, and remote-operated vehicles (ROVs).

B. **The Need for Non-Invasive Techniques:** Submerged archaeological sites are often delicate and sensitive to disturbance. Non-invasive remote sensing methods are preferred to minimize the risk of damage.

C. **Imaging and Data Collection:** Remote sensing tools generate images and data that can be used to create maps, 3D models, and assess the composition of underwater sites.

D. **Challenges of the Underwater Environment:** The underwater environment poses unique challenges, such as limited visibility, currents, and the need for specialized equipment to conduct remote sensing.

## II. Methods and Data Acquisition:

A. **Sonar Technology:** Sonar systems emit sound waves and measure their return time to create detailed images of underwater features, including shipwrecks and submerged landscapes.

B. **Magnetometry:** Magnetometers detect variations in the Earth's magnetic field caused by ferrous materials, which can help locate shipwrecks and submerged structures.

C. **Photogrammetry:** Underwater photogrammetry involves capturing high-resolution images of archaeological sites and artifacts, which are then processed to create 3D models.

D. **ROVs and AUVs:** Remote-operated vehicles (ROVs) and autonomous underwater vehicles (AUVs) equipped with cameras and sensors are used to explore and document underwater sites. ROVs can be operated remotely, while AUVs are autonomous and follow pre-programmed paths.

## III. Applications of Remote Sensing in Underwater Archaeology:

A. **Site Discovery and Mapping:** Remote sensing methods are used to locate and map submerged shipwrecks, ancient harbors, and underwater settlements.

B. **Archaeological Site Characterization:** Sonar and magnetometry provide data on the composition and layout of underwater archaeological sites.

C. **Virtual Reconstruction:** Data collected through photogrammetry and 3D modeling contribute to the virtual reconstruction of shipwrecks and submerged structures.

D. **Cultural Heritage Preservation:** Remote sensing aids in documenting and preserving submerged cultural heritage by creating detailed records for conservation and research.

E. **Environmental Impact Assessment:** Remote sensing techniques are used to assess the environmental impact of underwater construction projects and industrial activities on archaeological sites.

**IV. Case Studies:**

A. **Antikythera Shipwreck, Greece:** Remote sensing technology was employed to explore and document the Antikythera shipwreck, uncovering the famous Antikythera Mechanism and a treasure trove of ancient artifacts.

B. **Port Royal, Jamaica:** Remote sensing played a crucial role in mapping the sunken city of Port Royal, providing insights into its layout and historical significance.

**V. Challenges and Future Directions:**

A. **Data Interpretation:** Interpreting remote sensing data from underwater sites requires expertise and can be complex due to the unique conditions of the underwater environment.

B. **Technology Advancements:** Continual advancements in remote sensing technology, including high-resolution imaging, automation, and improved underwater communication systems, hold promise for the future of underwater archaeology.

C. **Interdisciplinary Collaboration:** Effective remote sensing in underwater archaeology often necessitates collaboration between archaeologists, marine scientists, and engineers.

D. **Conservation and Preservation:** Balancing the exploration of underwater archaeological sites with their conservation and protection is an ongoing challenge.

E. **Environmental Concerns:** The impact of underwater archaeology and remote sensing activities on the underwater environment and ecosystems requires careful consideration.

In summary, remote sensing is a transformative technology that has opened new horizons in underwater archaeology. It enables the discovery, mapping, and documentation of submerged cultural heritage, shedding light on our maritime history and the secrets hidden beneath the world's waters. As technology continues to evolve and interdisciplinary collaborations expand, the future of remote sensing in underwater archaeology promises to reveal more about our shared human past and the submerged mysteries waiting to be uncovered.

# CHAPTER 17: REMOTE SENSING FOR CLIMATE AND ENVIRONMENTAL STUDIES

Remote sensing is a crucial tool for climate and environmental studies, providing a means to collect valuable data about the Earth's atmosphere, oceans, land, and ecosystems from a distance. This technology employs a variety of sensors and platforms, including satellites, drones, and ground-based instruments, to monitor and assess various environmental parameters, which are essential for understanding climate change, natural resource management, disaster monitoring, and ecological conservation. In this comprehensive exploration of remote sensing for climate and environmental studies, we will delve into the fundamental principles, methods, applications, case studies, challenges, and the transformative impact it has had on our ability to monitor and protect our planet.

**I. Fundamental Principles:**

A. **What is Remote Sensing in Climate and Environmental Studies?** Remote sensing is the science of acquiring information about the Earth and its surroundings from a distance, typically using sensors mounted on aircraft, satellites, drones, or ground-based instruments. It involves the measurement of various electromagnetic radiation properties, such as reflected sunlight, emitted thermal radiation, and radio waves, to obtain environmental data.

B. **Electromagnetic Spectrum:** The electromagnetic spectrum includes a wide range of wavelengths, from visible light to microwave and radio waves. Different regions of this spectrum are used for specific remote sensing applications. For instance, visible and infrared wavelengths are used for vegetation monitoring, while microwave is employed for soil moisture and ocean surface observations.

C. **Sensors and Platforms:** Remote sensing utilizes a variety of sensors, such as optical cameras, thermal infrared sensors, radar systems, and spectrometers. These sensors can be mounted on satellites orbiting the Earth, aircraft flying at different altitudes, drones, or ground-based stations.

D. **Data Acquisition and Processing:** Remote sensing data are acquired by the sensors and transmitted to ground stations for processing. This data is then converted into meaningful information through image processing, data analysis, and modeling.

## II. Methods and Data Acquisition:

A. **Satellite Remote Sensing:** Satellites provide a global perspective on the Earth's climate and environment. Platforms like NASA's MODIS and the European Space Agency's Sentinel missions continuously collect data on land, ocean, and atmospheric parameters.

B. **Aerial Remote Sensing:** Aerial surveys using aircraft are valuable for collecting high-resolution data for localized studies, such as land use mapping and vegetation health assessments.

C. **Drone-based Remote Sensing:** Drones, or Unmanned Aerial Vehicles (UAVs), are increasingly used for environmental monitoring due to their versatility and the ability to capture data at different spatial resolutions.

D. **Ground-based Remote Sensing:** Ground-based instruments, such as weather stations, radiometers, and LiDAR (Light Detection and Ranging) devices, are essential for collecting data close to the Earth's surface.

## III. Applications of Remote Sensing in Climate and Environmental Studies:

A. **Climate Change Monitoring:** Remote sensing provides

essential data on key climate change indicators like temperature, sea level rise, glacial melt, and greenhouse gas concentrations.

B. **Weather Forecasting:** Satellite data are crucial for weather prediction and monitoring extreme weather events, allowing early warnings and disaster preparedness.

C. **Natural Resource Management:** Remote sensing assists in the sustainable management of natural resources, including forestry, agriculture, water resources, and fisheries.

D. **Ecosystem Monitoring:** Satellites monitor ecosystems, tracking changes in land cover, vegetation health, and biodiversity to inform conservation efforts.

E. **Ocean and Coastal Studies:** Remote sensing plays a critical role in monitoring sea surface temperature, ocean currents, and coastal erosion, helping to protect coastlines and marine environments.

F. **Disaster Response and Recovery:** Remote sensing aids in disaster management by assessing damage caused by earthquakes, floods, wildfires, and other natural disasters.

G. **Air and Water Quality Monitoring:** Remote sensing provides data on air pollution, water quality, and the distribution of harmful algal blooms.

**IV. Case Studies:**

A. **Monitoring Deforestation in the Amazon:** Satellite imagery has been crucial for monitoring deforestation and illegal logging in the Amazon rainforest, contributing to conservation efforts.

B. **Hurricane Tracking and Prediction:** Satellites provide real-time data to track the development and path of hurricanes, enabling accurate predictions and timely response to potential disasters.

**V. Challenges and Future Directions:**

A. **Data Interpretation and Analysis:** Interpreting remote sensing data can be complex, requiring advanced techniques and models for meaningful information extraction.

B. **Data Resolution and Spatial Coverage:** Balancing spatial coverage and data resolution is a challenge. High-resolution data often cover limited areas, while lower-resolution data can cover vast regions.

C. **Integration of Multi-Sensor Data:** Combining data from different sensors and platforms can be challenging but is necessary for comprehensive environmental studies.

D. **Calibration and Validation:** Ensuring the accuracy and reliability of remote sensing data requires thorough calibration and validation processes.

E. **Technological Advancements:** Advancements in sensor technology, including hyperspectral sensors, improved data storage, and data analysis techniques, will shape the future of remote sensing.

In summary, remote sensing is a transformative technology for climate and environmental studies, playing a critical role in monitoring climate change, natural resources, ecosystems, and disasters. It provides essential data for informed decision-making, environmental protection, and disaster response. As technology continues to advance and remote sensing becomes more integrated with other Earth observation systems, it promises to play an increasingly vital role in safeguarding our planet and addressing the complex challenges of climate and environmental conservation.

# CHAPTER 18: SOIL ANALYSIS FOR ARCHAEOLOGICAL SITE DETECTION

Soil analysis is a fundamental and multifaceted tool in the field of archaeology, particularly in the detection and exploration of archaeological sites. The study of soil and sediment properties can reveal hidden archaeological features, artifacts, and the past activities of ancient civilizations. In this extensive exploration of soil analysis for archaeological site detection, we will delve into the fundamental principles, methods, applications, case studies, challenges, and the transformative impact it has had on our understanding of the past.

**I. Fundamental Principles:**

A. **Why is Soil Analysis Important in Archaeology?** Soil analysis in archaeology involves the examination of soil composition, texture, color, and other physical properties to locate and characterize archaeological sites. These properties can indicate human activities, such as construction, burial, or occupation.

B. **Soil as a Historical Record:** Soil layers can preserve a chronological record of past human activities, including building foundations, hearths, garbage pits, and burials. These layers are stratified, with older deposits at lower depths and younger ones near the surface.

C. **Pedology and Soil Science:** Soil analysis draws on principles from pedology (the study of soil in its natural environment) and soil science to understand the formation and characteristics of archaeological soils.

D. **Multi-disciplinary Approach:** Archaeologists often collaborate with soil scientists, geologists, and geomorphologists to interpret soil data in the context of archaeological investigations.

## II. Methods and Data Acquisition:

A. **Soil Sampling:** Archaeologists collect soil samples from potential archaeological sites using various methods, such as augering, coring, and excavation. Samples are taken at various depths and locations to capture the variability of soil properties.

B. **Laboratory Analysis:** Soil samples are analyzed in the laboratory for properties like texture, pH, organic content, mineral composition, and chemical residues. Specialized techniques, such as micromorphology and geoarchaeology, are employed to examine soil microstructures and sedimentary layers.

C. **Geophysical Methods:** Ground-penetrating radar (GPR) and electrical resistivity surveying are geophysical techniques that can complement soil analysis by providing subsurface information without excavation.

D. **Remote Sensing:** Remote sensing technologies like aerial photography and LiDAR can reveal subtle changes in vegetation and topography that indicate archaeological features beneath the soil.

## III. Applications of Soil Analysis in Archaeological Site Detection:

A. **Site Location and Verification:** Soil analysis aids in the identification and verification of archaeological sites. Discrepancies in soil characteristics can indicate the presence of features like walls, ditches, or hearths.

B. **Delineation of Features:** Archaeologists use soil analysis to define the boundaries and characteristics of features within a site, helping to map and interpret the layout of ancient settlements or structures.

C. **Cultural Stratigraphy:** Soil analysis assists in establishing the cultural stratigraphy of a site, revealing the sequence of human occupation and activities over time.

D. **Dating and Chronology:** By examining soil layers and their contents, archaeologists can establish relative and absolute dating of archaeological contexts.

E. **Artifact Preservation:** Certain soil conditions, such as low oxygen levels or acidic pH, can preserve organic materials, such as wood, leather, and textiles, for millennia.

**IV. Case Studies:**

A. **Catalhoyuk, Turkey:** The archaeological site of Çatalhöyük, known for its well-preserved Neolithic houses and artifacts, extensively used soil analysis to understand the site's history and social organization.

B. **Teotihuacan, Mexico:** Soil analysis played a crucial role in uncovering the ancient city of Teotihuacan, its layout, and its urban planning principles.

**V. Challenges and Future Directions:**

A. **Interpretation Complexity:** Interpreting soil data can be complex and requires expertise, as soil properties can vary due to natural processes and anthropogenic activities.

B. **Destruction of Sites:** The excavation process itself can be destructive to archaeological sites, so non-invasive methods like geophysics and remote sensing are increasingly favored.

C. **Environmental Considerations:** Archaeologists must consider the environmental and ethical implications of soil sampling and excavation, especially in sensitive or protected areas.

D. **Technology Integration:** The integration of soil analysis with other technologies like geophysics and remote sensing holds promise for more comprehensive site detection and characterization.

E. **Public Outreach:** Efforts to engage local communities and the public in archaeological soil analysis can raise awareness and support for site conservation and research.

In summary, soil analysis is a critical tool in archaeological site detection, aiding in the location, mapping, and interpretation of archaeological features and contexts. It is essential for uncovering the mysteries of ancient civilizations, understanding their activities, and preserving our shared human heritage. As technology and interdisciplinary collaboration continue to advance, soil analysis will play an increasingly important role in unraveling the past and informing our understanding of the history and cultures that have come before us.

# CHAPTER 19: GEOPHYSICAL SURVEY TECHNIQUES IN ARCHAEOLOGY

Geophysical survey techniques have become invaluable tools in archaeological research, revolutionizing the way we explore, map, and interpret archaeological sites. These non-invasive methods enable archaeologists to "see" beneath the ground without excavation, offering insights into buried structures, artifacts, and cultural landscapes. In this comprehensive exploration of geophysical survey techniques in archaeology, we will delve into the fundamental principles, methods, applications, case studies, challenges, and the transformative impact they have had on our understanding of the past.

**I. Fundamental Principles:**

A. **Why Geophysics in Archaeology?** Geophysical survey techniques involve the measurement of physical properties of the subsurface, such as magnetic susceptibility, electrical conductivity, ground-penetrating radar (GPR) reflections, and resistivity. These properties can reveal archaeological features and anomalies without disturbing the site.

B. **Non-Invasive Nature:** Geophysical methods are non-invasive, minimizing damage to archaeological sites, and are particularly useful for areas where excavation is not practical or ethical.

C. **Ground as a Recorder:** Archaeologists consider the ground as a recorder of human activities. Buried features, such as walls, ditches, and hearths, can alter the physical properties of the soil, making them detectable with geophysical methods.

D. **Complementary Techniques:** Different geophysical methods provide unique information. Combining several techniques can improve the accuracy and interpretation of results.

## II. Methods and Data Acquisition:

A. **Magnetic Survey:** Magnetic survey measures variations in the Earth's magnetic field caused by buried structures or artifacts with magnetic properties. Iron objects, kilns, and hearths are often detected through magnetic anomalies.

B. **Electrical Resistivity Survey:** Electrical resistivity measures the ability of the ground to conduct electricity. Changes in resistivity can indicate features like walls, pits, and ditches, which affect the electrical flow.

C. **Ground-Penetrating Radar (GPR):** GPR sends electromagnetic waves into the ground and records reflections, allowing the detection of subsurface anomalies like walls, graves, and changes in soil stratigraphy.

D. **Electromagnetic Induction:** Electromagnetic induction measures the ground's electrical conductivity and is used to detect subsurface features, especially those associated with metal objects.

E. **Seismic Survey:** Seismic methods involve generating seismic waves and measuring their reflections. These techniques can reveal subsurface structures and stratigraphy.

F. **Gradiometry:** Gradiometers measure variations in the Earth's magnetic field and are particularly effective for detecting small-scale features like postholes and pits.

## III. Applications of Geophysical Survey Techniques in Archaeology:

A. **Site Detection and Mapping:** Geophysical surveys help locate archaeological sites, map their extent, and identify features like walls, roads, and buildings.

B. **Site Characterization:** These techniques provide data on the size, layout, and depth of features, aiding in site characterization and interpretation.

C. **Stratigraphic Analysis:** Geophysics assists in understanding the stratigraphy of sites, revealing chronological sequences of human occupation.

D. **Anomaly Identification:** Archaeologists use geophysical data to identify anomalies that may indicate the presence of buried objects, tombs, or architectural remains.

E. **Monitoring and Preservation:** Geophysics can be used to monitor the condition of archaeological sites and assess the impact of development or natural processes on buried features.

**IV. Case Studies:**

A. **Pompeii, Italy:** Geophysical surveys have played a vital role in uncovering the layout of the ancient city of Pompeii, preserving its fragile remains and enabling the study of daily life in the Roman Empire.

B. **Stonehenge, United Kingdom:** Geophysical techniques have contributed to a better understanding of the Stonehenge landscape, revealing the presence of previously unknown monuments and structures.

**V. Challenges and Future Directions:**

A. **Interpretation Complexity:** Interpreting geophysical data requires expertise and experience, as features may have different effects on multiple properties.

B. **Environmental Factors:** Weather conditions, the type of soil, and vegetation cover can impact the effectiveness of geophysical surveys.

C. **Calibration and Validation:** Ensuring the accuracy and reliability of geophysical data is essential, often requiring ground-truthing through excavation.

D. **Public Awareness and Outreach:** Engaging the public and local communities in the value of geophysical methods and archaeological research is important for site preservation and awareness.

E. **Advancements in Technology:** Continual advancements

in geophysical instruments, software, and data processing techniques hold promise for the future of archaeological research.

In summary, geophysical survey techniques have revolutionized archaeological research by providing non-invasive means of detecting, mapping, and characterizing archaeological sites and features. They enable archaeologists to explore the past without disturbing the present, uncovering the mysteries of ancient civilizations and preserving our shared human heritage. As technology advances and interdisciplinary collaboration expands, geophysics promises to play an increasingly important role in advancing our understanding of the past and shaping the future of archaeology.

# CHAPTER 20: ARCHAEOLOGICAL APPLICATIONS OF SPECTROSCOPY

Spectroscopy is a powerful analytical technique with a wide range of applications across various scientific fields, including archaeology. It involves the interaction of matter with electromagnetic radiation, allowing scientists to study the composition and properties of materials. In archaeology, spectroscopy has emerged as an essential tool for non-destructive analysis, dating, provenance determination, and the study of ancient artifacts, enabling a deeper understanding of past civilizations and their material culture. In this comprehensive exploration of the archaeological applications of spectroscopy, we will delve into the fundamental principles, methods, applications, case studies, challenges, and the transformative impact this technique has had on our understanding of ancient civilizations.

## I. Fundamental Principles:

A. **What is Spectroscopy?** Spectroscopy is the study of the interaction between matter and electromagnetic radiation. It allows researchers to identify elements, compounds, and minerals based on the unique spectral characteristics of their atomic or molecular structure.

B. **Energy Levels and Spectral Lines:** When matter interacts with radiation, electrons in atoms or molecules move between energy levels, emitting or absorbing specific wavelengths of light. These transitions produce spectral lines that are characteristic of the material.

C. **Spectral Range:** Spectroscopy covers a wide range of the electromagnetic spectrum, from X-rays and ultraviolet (UV) to visible light, infrared (IR), and radio waves, with each region providing different types of information about the material being analyzed.

D. **Non-Destructive Nature:** One of the key advantages of spectroscopy in archaeology is its non-destructive nature. It allows for the analysis of artifacts and materials without damaging or altering them.

## II. Methods and Data Acquisition:

A. **X-ray Fluorescence (XRF):** XRF spectroscopy is widely used in archaeology to determine the elemental composition of artifacts and archaeological materials. It is especially valuable for identifying pigments on ancient ceramics and analyzing metal alloys.

B. **Visible and Infrared Spectroscopy:** Visible and infrared spectroscopy reveal information about the molecular composition of materials. These methods are employed for the analysis of ancient paints, dyes, and organic residues on artifacts.

C. **Raman Spectroscopy:** Raman spectroscopy is used to identify minerals and pigments in archaeological materials. It provides information about the crystalline structure of compounds and is valuable for studying pottery, pigments, and gems.

D. **UV-Visible Spectroscopy:** UV-Visible spectroscopy is used to study the electronic structure of materials. It can help identify colorants in archaeological artifacts like glass, ceramics, and ancient textiles.

## III. Applications of Spectroscopy in Archaeology:

A. **Provenance and Sourcing:** Spectroscopy is employed to determine the geological or geographical origin of archaeological materials, such as ceramics, metals, and lithics. This is essential for understanding trade networks and cultural interactions.

B. **Dating and Chronology:** Luminescence dating, a technique that uses the energy stored in minerals, is a form of spectroscopy used to establish the age of archaeological materials, such as pottery and sediments.

C. **Paint and Pigment Analysis:** Spectroscopy is instrumental in identifying pigments and dyes used in ancient artworks and artifacts. This information helps in the reconstruction of ancient color palettes.

D. **Archaeobotany and Organic Residue Analysis:** Infrared spectroscopy is applied to analyze ancient plant remains and organic residues on ceramics, providing insights into past diets and food processing.

E. **Metal Composition Analysis:** XRF spectroscopy is frequently used to analyze the elemental composition of metal artifacts, helping to identify metal sources and alloying techniques.

F. **Gemstone Identification:** Spectroscopy is vital for identifying the mineral composition of gemstones used in ancient jewelry and ornaments.

## IV. Case Studies:

A. **Maya Blue Pigment:** Spectroscopy helped uncover the secrets of the Maya Blue pigment, revealing its unique chemical composition and the process used to create it.

B. **Pompeii Frescoes:** Spectroscopic analysis of pigments in Pompeii frescoes revealed the use of various materials and techniques in Roman wall paintings.

## V. Challenges and Future Directions:

A. **Complex Interpretation:** Interpreting spectroscopic data can be complex, requiring expertise and reference databases for accurate material identification.

B. **Sampling:** Even though spectroscopy is non-destructive, some applications require micro-sampling, which must be carefully managed to minimize any impact on artifacts.

C. **Interdisciplinary Collaboration:** Successful archaeological spectroscopy often involves collaboration with materials scientists, chemists, and other specialists.

D. **Advancements in Technology:** Continual advancements in spectroscopic instrumentation, including portable and handheld devices, are expanding its use in the field.

E. **Data Integration:** The integration of spectroscopic data with other analytical techniques and data, such as imaging and elemental analysis, enhances the overall understanding of archaeological materials.

In summary, spectroscopy is a transformative tool in archaeology, providing non-destructive insights into the composition and properties of ancient materials and artifacts. It contributes to our understanding of ancient civilizations, their technologies, and their cultural practices. As technology continues to advance and interdisciplinary collaboration expands, spectroscopy promises to play an increasingly important role in reshaping our understanding of the past and preserving our shared cultural heritage.

# CHAPTER 21: SPACEBORNE SAR IN CULTURAL HERITAGE PRESERVATION

Spaceborne Synthetic Aperture Radar (SAR) is a cutting-edge technology that has revolutionized the field of cultural heritage preservation and archaeological research. SAR, an active remote sensing technique, has the unique ability to capture high-resolution images of the Earth's surface regardless of weather conditions, day or night. In this extensive exploration of spaceborne SAR in cultural heritage preservation, we will delve into the fundamental principles, methods, applications, case studies, challenges, and the transformative impact it has had on our ability to safeguard and study our cultural heritage.

**I. Fundamental Principles:**

A. **What is Spaceborne SAR?** Spaceborne SAR is a remote sensing technology that uses radar waves to capture high-resolution images of the Earth's surface. Unlike passive optical sensors, SAR instruments can operate day and night and penetrate cloud cover, making them highly reliable for monitoring and preserving cultural heritage sites.

B. **Radar Imaging Process:** SAR instruments emit microwave pulses toward the Earth's surface and measure the return signals. By processing the radar echoes, SAR creates detailed images of surface features, including buildings, landscapes, and archaeological sites.

C. **Resolution and Sensitivity:** SAR provides high-resolution images with the ability to detect small changes in the Earth's surface. This is crucial for monitoring cultural heritage sites with precision.

D. **Temporal and Geospatial Coverage:** Spaceborne SAR systems, typically mounted on satellites, offer global coverage, enabling the monitoring of cultural heritage sites around the world.

## II. Methods and Data Acquisition:

A. **SAR Satellite Systems:** Various SAR satellite systems orbit the Earth, including those operated by organizations like the European Space Agency (ESA), NASA, and private companies like TerraSAR-X and Cosmo-Skymed. These systems vary in terms of spatial resolution and imaging modes.

B. **Imaging Modes:** SAR instruments offer different imaging modes, including StripMap, Spotlight, and Interferometric SAR (InSAR), each with its own advantages for cultural heritage preservation.

C. **Interferometric SAR (InSAR):** InSAR is a specialized technique that uses SAR images to detect millimeter-level ground movements, which is valuable for monitoring the stability of cultural heritage structures.

D. **Multitemporal Analysis:** SAR images can be acquired over time, allowing for the detection of changes in cultural heritage sites, such as subsidence, vegetation growth, or illegal excavations.

## III. Applications of Spaceborne SAR in Cultural Heritage Preservation:

A. **Site Monitoring and Preservation:** SAR technology is used to monitor the structural stability and conservation status of cultural heritage sites, including historic buildings, archaeological ruins, and cultural landscapes.

B. **Environmental Impact Assessment:** SAR helps assess the impact of natural disasters, climate change, and urban development on cultural heritage sites.

C. **Site Detection and Mapping:** SAR assists in the discovery and mapping of hidden archaeological sites, including buried structures and landscapes.

D. **Documentation of Cultural Landscapes:** SAR captures detailed images of cultural landscapes, such as ancient roads, irrigation systems, and agricultural terraces.

E. **Inventory and Documentation:** Cultural heritage sites can be inventoried and documented with high-resolution SAR imagery, aiding in heritage preservation and research.

## IV. Case Studies:

A. **Angkor, Cambodia:** Spaceborne SAR has been used to monitor the condition of the Angkor archaeological complex, revealing information about the stability of the ancient temples and identifying previously unknown structures.

B. **Pompeii, Italy:** SAR technology has been employed to study the subsidence and structural changes of the ancient city of Pompeii, which is crucial for its preservation and protection.

## V. Challenges and Future Directions:

A. **Data Processing and Interpretation:** SAR data processing can be complex, requiring specialized software and expertise in radar remote sensing.

B. **Temporal Resolution:** The revisit time of SAR satellites can affect the ability to monitor dynamic changes at cultural heritage sites.

C. **Accessibility and Cost:** Access to SAR data and the associated costs can be barriers for some researchers and heritage preservation organizations.

D. **Integration with Other Technologies:** Combining SAR data with other remote sensing technologies, such as LiDAR and optical imagery, enhances the analysis of cultural heritage sites.

E. **Capacity Building:** Education and training in SAR technology are essential for building local capacity for cultural heritage preservation in many regions.

In summary, spaceborne SAR has transformed cultural heritage preservation by offering an unprecedented ability to monitor, document, and protect heritage sites on a global scale. Its non-invasive, all-weather capabilities are invaluable for safeguarding our cultural heritage from environmental threats and ensuring the continued study of our shared history. As technology continues to advance and access to SAR data becomes more widespread, the future of cultural heritage preservation is poised to benefit significantly from this transformative technology.

# CHAPTER 22: REMOTE SENSING IN CULTURAL HERITAGE CONSERVATION

Remote sensing, a powerful technology employed in a variety of fields, has become a pivotal tool in cultural heritage conservation and archaeology. It involves the collection and interpretation of data from a distance, enabling experts to study and preserve historical sites, artifacts, and cultural landscapes. This comprehensive exploration of remote sensing in cultural heritage conservation will delve into the fundamental principles, methods, applications, case studies, challenges, and the transformative impact it has had on preserving our shared cultural heritage.

## I. Fundamental Principles:

A. **What is Remote Sensing in Cultural Heritage Conservation?** Remote sensing involves the use of sensors, instruments, and technology to capture data about cultural heritage sites and artifacts without physical contact. It enables experts to study, document, and preserve historical and archaeological assets.

B. **Non-Invasive Nature:** Remote sensing techniques are non-invasive, meaning they do not disrupt or harm the cultural heritage objects and sites under investigation. This is crucial for conservation efforts.

C. **Data Collection and Interpretation:** Remote sensing technologies generate data that can be interpreted to create detailed records, maps, 3D models, and other valuable resources for conservation and research.

D. **Multi-Sensor and Multi-Temporal Approaches:** Combining data from different sensors and collecting data over various time periods can provide a more comprehensive understanding of cultural heritage sites and changes over time.

## II. Methods and Data Acquisition:

A. **Photogrammetry:** Photogrammetry involves capturing high-resolution images of cultural heritage objects and sites from multiple angles to create 3D models and orthophotos.

B. **LiDAR (Light Detection and Ranging):** LiDAR technology uses laser pulses to measure distances, creating precise 3D representations of cultural heritage sites, which are valuable for mapping and analysis.

C. **Aerial and Satellite Imagery:** Aerial and satellite images are crucial for surveying and documenting large-scale cultural landscapes and archaeological sites. They can reveal hidden features through variations in vegetation and terrain.

D. **Thermal Imaging:** Thermal imaging can help identify areas of deterioration or structural issues in cultural heritage structures by detecting variations in temperature.

E. **Ground-Penetrating Radar (GPR):** GPR is used to explore sub-surface structures and archaeological remains, providing non-invasive insights into the presence of hidden features.

## III. Applications of Remote Sensing in Cultural Heritage Conservation:

A. **Site Documentation and Mapping:** Remote sensing helps create accurate maps and 3D models of cultural heritage sites and artifacts for documentation and preservation.

B. **Structural Health Assessment:** It is used to assess the structural integrity of historical buildings and monuments and detect potential issues like cracks and deformations.

C. **Conservation Monitoring:** Remote sensing techniques aid in monitoring the condition of cultural heritage sites and detecting deterioration or damage, allowing for timely conservation efforts.

D. **Cultural Landscape Preservation:** Aerial imagery is essential for monitoring and preserving entire cultural landscapes, including historic gardens, agricultural terraces, and urban centers.

E. **Site Discovery and Exploration:** LiDAR and GPR are valuable for discovering new archaeological sites and exploring hidden features without excavation.

F. **Environmental Impact Assessment:** Remote sensing assesses the impact of natural disasters, climate change, and human activities on cultural heritage sites.

**IV. Case Studies:**

A. **Machu Picchu, Peru:** LiDAR technology has helped researchers uncover previously unknown structures and features in the ancient Incan city of Machu Picchu, contributing to its preservation and understanding.

B. **Angkor, Cambodia:** Remote sensing has played a significant role in studying and conserving the Angkor archaeological complex, including the famous Angkor Wat temple.

**V. Challenges and Future Directions:**

A. **Interpretation Complexity:** Interpreting remote sensing data, especially multi-sensor data, can be complex and requires expertise.

B. **Data Storage and Management:** Remote sensing generates vast amounts of data that need to be efficiently stored and managed.

C. **Accessibility and Cost:** Access to remote sensing data and technology can be a barrier for some conservation projects, particularly in developing regions.

D. **Community Engagement:** Engaging local communities and stakeholders in remote sensing projects and cultural heritage conservation is essential.

E. **Integration with Traditional Methods:** Balancing the benefits of remote sensing with traditional archaeological and conservation methods is a challenge but is crucial for successful projects.

In summary, remote sensing has transformed cultural heritage conservation and archaeology by providing non-invasive, detailed insights into historical sites, objects, and landscapes. It has revolutionized documentation, monitoring, and preservation efforts, contributing to a deeper understanding of our shared cultural heritage. As technology advances, accessibility increases, and interdisciplinary collaboration expands, the future of remote sensing in cultural heritage conservation promises to enhance our ability to safeguard and celebrate our rich and diverse history.

# CHAPTER 23: DIGITAL PRESERVATION OF ARCHAEOLOGICAL SITES

The digital preservation of archaeological sites is a multifaceted and innovative approach to safeguarding the cultural and historical heritage of past civilizations. It involves the use of digital technologies to record, document, and protect archaeological sites and artifacts from deterioration, destruction, or loss. This comprehensive exploration of digital preservation in archaeology will delve into the fundamental principles, methods, applications, case studies, challenges, and the transformative impact it has had on our ability to protect and study our shared human history.

**I. Fundamental Principles:**

A. **What is Digital Preservation in Archaeology?** Digital preservation in archaeology involves creating digital records, models, and databases of archaeological sites, features, artifacts, and cultural landscapes. These digital assets serve as a long-term record of the site and its context.

B. **Non-Destructive Nature:** Digital preservation is non-invasive and does not harm the original archaeological materials. It complements traditional excavation and conservation methods.

C. **Data Management:** Managing and curating digital data is a fundamental aspect of digital preservation. Effective data management ensures the accessibility, integrity, and longevity of digital records.

D. **Interdisciplinary Collaboration:** Digital preservation requires collaboration between archaeologists, conservators, geospatial experts, and digital specialists to capture and preserve diverse types of archaeological data.

**II. Methods and Data Acquisition:**

A. **3D Scanning and Photogrammetry:** 3D scanning and photogrammetry techniques create highly accurate 3D models of artifacts, structures, and landscapes. These models can be used for analysis and virtual reconstruction.

B. **Geospatial Technologies:** Geographic Information Systems (GIS) and GPS are used to create spatial databases of archaeological sites and features, enabling precise mapping and monitoring.

C. **Photography and Image Archives:** Photography and image archives document the condition of archaeological sites and artifacts over time, aiding in conservation and research.

D. **Digital Documentation and Databases:** Archaeologists create digital records and databases of artifacts, stratigraphy, and excavation notes. These databases serve as comprehensive references for research and conservation.

E. **Augmented Reality (AR) and Virtual Reality (VR):** AR and VR technologies offer immersive experiences that enable users to explore archaeological sites and reconstructions digitally.

**III. Applications of Digital Preservation in Archaeology:**

A. **Conservation and Site Management:** Digital preservation aids in monitoring and conserving archaeological sites, preventing physical damage or deterioration.

B. **Data Sharing and Accessibility:** Digital data is easily shared and accessed by researchers, scholars, and the public, promoting open science and public engagement with cultural heritage.

C. **Education and Outreach:** Digital reconstructions and models make cultural heritage accessible to a broader audience, fostering educational initiatives and tourism.

D. **Research and Analysis:** Archaeologists use digital records for in-depth analysis, such as studying stratigraphy, examining artifact details, and exploring spatial relationships.

E. **Virtual Museums:** Virtual museum exhibits allow the public to explore artifacts and cultural heritage collections online.

**IV. Case Studies:**

A. **Cyber-archaeology in Egypt:** The Giza 3D project digitally preserves the Giza pyramids and the surrounding archaeological landscape, enabling researchers and the public to explore these iconic structures from anywhere in the world.

B. **Pompeii, Italy:** Digital preservation initiatives in Pompeii have created detailed digital models of the archaeological site, allowing experts to monitor the condition of the ancient city and develop better conservation strategies.

**V. Challenges and Future Directions:**

A. **Data Storage and Management:** The long-term preservation of digital data poses challenges, including data storage, format obsolescence, and metadata maintenance.

B. **Interoperability:** Ensuring that diverse digital tools and software can work together and that data can be easily shared is essential.

C. **Ethical and Legal Issues:** Digital preservation initiatives must address issues related to copyright, data ownership, and cultural sensitivities.

D. **Public Engagement:** Engaging the public in digital preservation initiatives and fostering a sense of stewardship for cultural heritage are ongoing challenges.

E. **Continual Technological Advancements:** Advancements in technology, such as 3D printing, artificial intelligence, and machine learning, offer exciting opportunities for digital preservation in archaeology.

In summary, digital preservation is a transformative approach to safeguarding and celebrating our shared human history. It enables the long-term protection of archaeological sites, artifacts, and cultural landscapes while also making this heritage accessible to a global audience. As technology continues to advance, digital preservation will play an increasingly important role in archaeological research, conservation, and education, ensuring that our cultural heritage endures for future generations.

# CHAPTER 24: UAV PHOTOGRAMMETRY IN SITE RECORDING

Unmanned Aerial Vehicles (UAVs), commonly known as drones, have rapidly evolved and found their place in a wide range of applications, including archaeological site recording. When combined with photogrammetry, a technique for obtaining measurements from photographs, UAVs offer a powerful tool for capturing high-resolution, detailed imagery of archaeological sites. This detailed imagery can then be transformed into accurate 3D models and maps for site recording, documentation, and analysis. In this extensive exploration of UAV photogrammetry in site recording, we will delve into the fundamental principles, methods, applications, case studies, challenges, and the transformative impact it has had on the field of archaeology.

**I. Fundamental Principles:**

A. **What is UAV Photogrammetry in Site Recording?** UAV photogrammetry involves the use of drones to capture a series of overlapping images of archaeological sites from the air. These images are then processed to create 2D maps or 3D models, providing detailed and accurate site records.

B. **Photogrammetry in Archaeology:** Photogrammetry is a method that uses photographs to obtain measurements and three-dimensional information about objects and scenes. In archaeology, it can be used for site recording, artifact analysis, and preservation efforts.

C. **High-Resolution Imagery:** UAVs equipped with high-resolution cameras can capture images with exceptional detail, enabling archaeologists to record even the smallest features of a site.

D. **Orthophoto and Digital Elevation Models (DEM):** Orthophotos are geometrically corrected aerial images, while DEMs represent the elevation of the terrain. These products are key outcomes of UAV photogrammetry and are valuable for site documentation.

## II. Methods and Data Acquisition:

A. **UAV Equipment:** UAVs used in archaeological site recording are typically equipped with high-quality cameras, GPS systems, and autopilot software for autonomous flight and image capture.

B. **Image Capture:** UAVs fly predefined flight paths, capturing images with significant overlap to ensure accurate 3D modeling. These images are taken from various angles and elevations.

C. **Ground Control Points (GCPs):** GCPs are known reference points on the ground, with accurately measured coordinates. They are essential for georeferencing and scaling the imagery.

D. **Image Processing Software:** Specialized software, like Structure-from-Motion (SfM) and Multi-View Stereo (MVS) algorithms, are used to process the images and create 3D models and orthophotos.

## III. Applications of UAV Photogrammetry in Site Recording:

A. **Site Documentation and Mapping:** UAV photogrammetry is used to create highly accurate and detailed maps of archaeological sites. This aids in site documentation and preservation.

B. **3D Modeling:** UAVs can generate 3D models of archaeological features, buildings, and landscapes. These models are instrumental for analysis and interpretation.

C. **Artifact Analysis:** UAV photogrammetry can be used to create 3D models of artifacts, enabling detailed analysis without physical contact.

D. **Monitoring and Conservation:** Archaeologists use UAVs to monitor site conditions and the impact of environmental factors and human activities, aiding in conservation efforts.

E. **Georeferencing:** UAV imagery can be georeferenced and integrated with GIS systems, providing spatial context and data for broader archaeological research.

## IV. Case Studies:

A. **Nazca Lines, Peru:** UAV photogrammetry has been employed to document and monitor the Nazca Lines, intricate geoglyphs etched into the Peruvian desert.

B. **Orkney, Scotland:** UAVs have aided in the detailed mapping and analysis of ancient Neolithic sites in Orkney, shedding light on the architectural features and spatial layout of these structures.

## V. Challenges and Future Directions:

A. **Data Processing Complexity:** Processing large volumes of high-resolution images can be time-consuming and computationally demanding.

B. **Regulatory Compliance:** Obtaining the necessary permits and adhering to aviation regulations can be a challenge for UAV-based archaeological research.

C. **Data Storage and Management:** Handling, storing, and sharing the vast amount of data generated by UAV photogrammetry require efficient data management strategies.

D. **Public Engagement:** Engaging the public in archaeological research and demonstrating the value of UAV photogrammetry in cultural heritage conservation is essential.

E. **Continual Technological Advancements:** Advancements in UAV technology, such as improved sensors and data processing algorithms, will continue to enhance the capabilities of UAV photogrammetry.

In summary, UAV photogrammetry has transformed

archaeological site recording and documentation by providing highly detailed and accurate imagery for analysis and preservation. It is a non-invasive, efficient, and cost-effective method that complements traditional archaeological fieldwork. As technology advances and interdisciplinary collaboration expands, the future of UAV photogrammetry promises to further revolutionize archaeological research and conservation efforts, ensuring the preservation of our shared human heritage for future generations.

# CHAPTER 25: THERMAL INFRARED IMAGING FOR BURIED FEATURES

Thermal infrared imaging, a non-invasive remote sensing technique, has emerged as a valuable tool in archaeology for detecting and studying buried features. This method utilizes the temperature differences between the surface and subsurface to reveal hidden archaeological structures and artifacts. In this comprehensive exploration of thermal infrared imaging for buried features, we will delve into the fundamental principles, methods, applications, case studies, challenges, and the transformative impact it has had on our understanding of ancient civilizations.

**I. Fundamental Principles:**

A. **What is Thermal Infrared Imaging?** Thermal infrared imaging, also known as thermography, involves the use of thermal cameras to capture the infrared radiation emitted by objects. These cameras detect temperature differences and generate thermal images, often represented in false-color scales.

B. **Thermal Differences in Archaeological Contexts:** Buried archaeological features, such as walls, ditches, and structures, can retain heat differently from the surrounding soil. This results in temperature contrasts that thermal cameras can detect.

C. **Thermal Inertia:** The ability of materials to retain and release heat, known as thermal inertia, plays a crucial role in the detection of buried features. High thermal inertia materials, like stone, can remain warmer or cooler than the surrounding soil, making them detectable.

D. **Day and Night Operation:** Thermal imaging is not dependent on natural light and can be conducted during both day and night, making it a versatile technique for archaeological investigations.

**II. Methods and Data Acquisition:**

A. **Thermal Cameras:** Thermal cameras, also called infrared cameras or thermographic cameras, capture thermal images by measuring the infrared radiation emitted by objects. They are available in various forms, including handheld devices and aerial-mounted systems.

B. **Temperature Differences:** Thermal cameras detect temperature differences on the Earth's surface and convert them into visual representations, usually employing a false-color scale to highlight the variations.

C. **Aerial and Ground-Based Surveys:** Thermal imaging can be conducted from the air using drones or aircraft, or from the ground by handheld cameras or vehicle-mounted systems.

D. **Thermal Data Processing:** Specialized software processes thermal data and creates thermal images. Data analysis techniques help identify anomalies that may indicate buried features.

**III. Applications of Thermal Infrared Imaging for Buried Features:**

A. **Site Discovery and Mapping:** Thermal infrared imaging helps in the identification and mapping of archaeological sites by revealing the presence of buried structures, walls, and features.

B. **Structural Assessment:** Thermography can assess the condition of historical buildings, detecting hidden structural issues or heat-related problems that affect conservation.

C. **Environmental Studies:** Thermal imaging is used to study the impact of climate change, vegetation, and subsurface conditions on archaeological sites.

D. **Water Management Systems:** Thermography aids in the identification of ancient irrigation or water management systems, which are often invisible on the surface.

E. **Geophysical Verification:** Thermal results can be combined with other geophysical methods, such as ground-penetrating radar (GPR) and magnetometry, to verify archaeological findings.

**IV. Case Studies:**

A. **Roman Villa, Italy:** Thermal infrared imaging has been employed to map the remains of a Roman villa in Italy. The temperature differences in the subsurface revealed the layout of the villa and its various rooms.

B. **Chaco Canyon, USA:** Thermography has been used to detect ancient subsurface structures and thermal anomalies in Chaco Canyon, providing insights into the architectural design and thermal properties of the structures.

**V. Challenges and Future Directions:**

A. **Interpretation Complexity:** Interpreting thermal images requires expertise, as anomalies can result from a variety of factors, including changes in thermal inertia, moisture content, and soil composition.

B. **Environmental Factors:** Weather conditions, soil moisture, and the time of day can impact the effectiveness of thermal imaging.

C. **Integration with Other Technologies:** Combining thermal imaging with other remote sensing methods and archaeological techniques enhances the accuracy of buried feature detection.

D. **Accessibility and Cost:** Thermal cameras and data processing can be expensive, limiting access for some archaeological projects.

E. **Continual Technological Advancements:** Ongoing advancements in thermal camera technology, data processing, and data analysis techniques hold promise for the future of thermal infrared imaging in archaeology.

In summary, thermal infrared imaging is a transformative tool in archaeology, offering a non-invasive means of detecting and mapping buried features, from ancient walls and structures to hidden water management systems. Its day and night operation and the ability to detect thermal anomalies make it a valuable addition to the archaeologist's toolkit. As technology continues to advance and interdisciplinary collaboration expands, thermal infrared imaging promises to play an increasingly important role in reshaping our understanding of the past and preserving our shared cultural heritage.

# CHAPTER 26: GIS-BASED ANALYSIS OF ANCIENT LANDSCAPES

Geographic Information Systems (GIS) have revolutionized the way we analyze and understand ancient landscapes. By combining spatial data, cartography, and various analytical tools, GIS allows archaeologists, historians, and researchers to unravel the complex relationships between human civilizations and their environments. In this extensive exploration of GIS-based analysis of ancient landscapes, we will delve into the fundamental principles, methods, applications, case studies, challenges, and the transformative impact it has had on our understanding of the past.

## I. Fundamental Principles:

A. **What is GIS?** GIS is a system that captures, stores, analyzes, and visualizes geographic information, such as maps, spatial data, and attributes. It allows for the integration of diverse datasets to better understand spatial relationships.

B. **Spatial Data:** Spatial data are the foundation of GIS, representing physical features and their attributes on the Earth's surface. These data can include maps, satellite imagery, GPS coordinates, and more.

C. **Geospatial Analysis:** GIS enables geospatial analysis, a process that involves examining spatial patterns, relationships, and trends to answer specific questions or solve problems.

D. **Historical GIS:** Historical GIS focuses on the application of GIS techniques to historical research, allowing for the analysis of past landscapes and the assessment of how they have changed over time.

## II. Methods and Data Acquisition:

A. **Geospatial Data Sources:** Data sources include maps, remote sensing imagery, aerial photography, LiDAR data, historical documents, and field surveys. These sources are often digitized and integrated into the GIS.

B. **Georeferencing:** Georeferencing involves assigning geographic coordinates to historical maps or documents, enabling their integration into the GIS and overlay with modern spatial data.

C. **Data Processing and Analysis:** GIS software is used for data processing and analysis. Geospatial operations include overlay, proximity analysis, spatial statistics, and network analysis.

D. **3D Visualization:** Advancements in GIS technology allow for 3D modeling and visualization of ancient landscapes, offering a more immersive understanding of past environments.

### III. Applications of GIS-Based Analysis of Ancient Landscapes:

A. **Settlement Patterns and Urban Planning:** GIS helps analyze the layout of ancient cities, the organization of streets, and the distribution of residential and commercial areas.

B. **Environmental Analysis:** It aids in the study of how ancient civilizations interacted with their environments, including land use, agricultural practices, and resource management.

C. **Archaeological Site Location:** GIS is instrumental in locating archaeological sites, predicting potential sites, and managing excavation and conservation efforts.

D. **Cultural Heritage Management:** It supports the preservation of cultural heritage by providing tools for site inventory, conservation planning, and monitoring.

E. **Route and Trade Analysis:** GIS can be used to analyze ancient trade routes, transportation networks, and the distribution of trade goods.

F. **Historical Mapping:** Creating historical maps with GIS allows researchers to visualize and understand changes in landscapes over time, such as urban growth or deforestation.

## IV. Case Studies:

A. **Pompeii, Italy:** GIS has been used to reconstruct the ancient city of Pompeii, mapping its streets, buildings, and infrastructure, and understanding how the city was organized.

B. **Angkor, Cambodia:** GIS has been employed to study the layout and development of the Angkor archaeological complex, revealing insights into the ancient Khmer Empire.

## V. Challenges and Future Directions:

A. **Data Integration:** Combining diverse datasets from different sources can be challenging, requiring careful data management and standardization.

B. **Historical Accuracy:** Historical maps and documents may have inaccuracies, and the process of georeferencing should consider these discrepancies.

C. **Interdisciplinary Collaboration:** Effective GIS-based analysis of ancient landscapes often involves collaboration with historians, archaeologists, geographers, and other specialists.

D. **Open Access and Data Sharing:** Sharing data and making research openly accessible is essential for the growth and impact of GIS-based research.

E. **Continual Technological Advancements:** As GIS technology evolves, it offers new tools and techniques for analyzing and visualizing ancient landscapes, paving the way for innovative research.

In summary, GIS-based analysis of ancient landscapes is a transformative approach to studying the past. It provides a multidimensional perspective on how ancient civilizations interacted with their environments and helps us uncover hidden patterns and relationships in historical data. As technology continues to advance and interdisciplinary collaboration expands, GIS-based research promises to play an increasingly important role in reshaping our understanding of ancient landscapes and the civilizations that shaped them.

# CHAPTER 27: REMOTE SENSING FOR ROCK ART DOCUMENTATION

Remote sensing techniques have greatly advanced the field of rock art documentation and research. Rock art, consisting of petroglyphs and pictographs, is an invaluable cultural heritage, providing insights into ancient civilizations, their belief systems, and artistic expressions. Remote sensing technologies help archaeologists and conservators record and study rock art sites in a non-invasive and non-destructive manner. In this comprehensive exploration of remote sensing for rock art documentation, we will delve into the fundamental principles, methods, applications, case studies, challenges, and the transformative impact it has had on the field of rock art studies.

**I. Fundamental Principles:**

A. **What is Rock Art?** Rock art comprises prehistoric or historic carvings and paintings on natural rock surfaces, often found in caves, shelters, and open landscapes. It includes petroglyphs (carvings) and pictographs (paintings).

B. **Importance of Rock Art:** Rock art serves as a significant cultural record, providing insights into the spiritual, cultural, and artistic practices of past civilizations.

C. **Non-Invasive Documentation:** Remote sensing for rock art documentation focuses on capturing imagery and data without physical contact with the rock art, which is crucial for preservation.

D. **Multidisciplinary Approach:** Rock art documentation often involves interdisciplinary collaboration between archaeologists, art historians, conservators, geologists, and remote sensing experts.

**II. Methods and Data Acquisition:**

A. **Aerial and Satellite Imaging:** Aerial and satellite imagery provides a broad overview of rock art sites, especially those located in open landscapes. They can reveal large-scale patterns and relationships.

B. **Photogrammetry:** Photogrammetry involves capturing a series of overlapping photographs from different angles to create accurate 3D models of rock art panels. This method aids in capturing fine details.

C. **Thermal Imaging:** Thermal cameras can detect temperature variations on rock surfaces, potentially revealing hidden petroglyphs or pictographs that are not visible to the naked eye.

D. **LiDAR (Light Detection and Ranging):** LiDAR technology uses laser pulses to create highly detailed 3D models of rock art and its surrounding landscape, helping to identify obscured features.

E. **Reflectance Spectroscopy:** Reflectance spectroscopy measures the way different materials reflect light. This technique can assist in identifying pigments and materials used in rock art paintings.

**III. Applications of Remote Sensing for Rock Art Documentation:**

A. **Site Mapping and Inventory:** Remote sensing aids in mapping and inventorying rock art sites, providing a comprehensive record of their locations.

B. **Damage Assessment:** Monitoring and documenting the condition of rock art helps in assessing potential damage or deterioration due to environmental factors or human activities.

C. **Hidden Art Detection:** Remote sensing can reveal hidden or faded rock art that is not visible to the naked eye, enhancing our understanding of the site.

D. **Rock Art Dating:** Analyzing rock surfaces with remote sensing methods can help establish the chronology of rock art creation.

E. **Preservation Planning:** Data from remote sensing informs preservation efforts and helps conservators determine the most appropriate methods for safeguarding rock art.

**IV. Case Studies:**

A. **Coso Range, California:** Remote sensing, including LiDAR and aerial photography, has been used to document the extensive petroglyphs in the Coso Range, California, shedding light on the complexity of the site.

B. **Lascaux Cave, France:** Reflectance spectroscopy has been employed to analyze the pigments used in the famous Lascaux Cave paintings, contributing to their preservation.

**V. Challenges and Future Directions:**

A. **Interpretation Complexity:** Interpreting remote sensing data for rock art can be complex, as it requires expertise in both remote sensing technology and rock art studies.

B. **Environmental Conditions:** Environmental factors, such as weather, lighting, and vegetation, can impact the effectiveness of remote sensing techniques.

C. **Public Access:** Balancing the need for site preservation and public access can be challenging when rock art sites are located in open landscapes.

D. **Integration with Traditional Methods:** Combining remote sensing data with traditional archaeological and rock art research methods is essential for a comprehensive understanding of these cultural treasures.

E. **Continual Technological Advancements:** As remote sensing technology evolves, new methods and sensors may emerge, offering further possibilities for rock art documentation and research.

In summary, remote sensing for rock art documentation is a transformative tool in preserving and understanding our ancient cultural heritage. It allows researchers to non-invasively capture and study these unique expressions of human creativity and spirituality. As technology advances, and as interdisciplinary collaboration expands, the future of remote sensing in rock art studies promises to enhance our ability to uncover, protect, and interpret the rich tapestry of rock art around the world.

# CHAPTER 28: MAGNETOMETRY IN ARCHAEOLOGICAL PROSPECTION

Magnetometry is a non-invasive geophysical method that has become an essential tool in the field of archaeology for investigating and understanding sub-surface archaeological features and anomalies. This technique involves measuring variations in the Earth's magnetic field caused by variations in the magnetic properties of the underlying materials. In this comprehensive exploration of magnetometry in archaeological prospection, we will delve into the fundamental principles, methods, applications, case studies, challenges, and the transformative impact it has had on archaeological research and site discovery.

## I. Fundamental Principles:

A. **Magnetic Properties of Archaeological Features:** Archaeological features, such as walls, hearths, pits, and ditches, can influence the magnetic properties of the soil around them. For example, burnt materials, like hearths or kilns, may exhibit high magnetic susceptibility, while stone structures can have a low susceptibility.

B. **Measuring Magnetic Variations:** Magnetometers measure the variations in the Earth's magnetic field, providing readings that can be influenced by the presence of archaeological features and materials.

C. **Non-Invasive Nature:** Magnetometry is a non-invasive technique, which means it does not require excavation and does not harm the archaeological site.

D. **Magnetic Anomalies:** Magnetometers record magnetic anomalies, which can be positive (enhanced magnetism, as in the case of fired materials) or negative (reduced magnetism, as in the case of voids or disturbances).

**II. Methods and Data Acquisition:**

A. **Magnetometers:** Magnetometers come in various types, including proton precession, fluxgate, and cesium vapor devices. These instruments measure magnetic fields with high sensitivity.

B. **Grid Surveys:** Archaeologists collect magnetometry data by systematically surveying a site on a grid, taking measurements at set intervals. This data is then used to create a magnetic map of the area.

C. **Data Processing:** The collected data is processed and analyzed to create magnetic maps that highlight anomalies. Specialized software helps identify and interpret these anomalies.

D. **Comparison with Other Data:** Magnetometry data is often combined with other archaeological survey techniques, such as ground-penetrating radar (GPR), to provide a more comprehensive understanding of sub-surface features.

**III. Applications of Magnetometry in Archaeological Prospection:**

A. **Site Discovery and Mapping:** Magnetometry is used to discover and map archaeological sites, including buried structures, roads, and enclosures.

B. **Feature Identification:** Archaeologists use magnetometry to identify specific features, like hearths, kilns, and postholes, within a site.

C. **Monitoring Site Integrity:** Magnetometry helps monitor the integrity of archaeological sites by detecting disturbances or looting activities.

D. **Landscape Analysis:** This technique contributes to the analysis of ancient landscapes, identifying patterns of human activity and settlement.

E. **Cemetery and Grave Detection:** Magnetometry has been

employed to locate and map burials and cemeteries, offering valuable insights into ancient burial practices.

**IV. Case Studies:**

A. **Roman Villa in Italy:** Magnetometry surveys of a Roman villa in Italy revealed the presence of walls, buildings, and courtyards, helping archaeologists understand the villa's layout and function.

B. **Iron Age Hillfort in the UK:** Magnetometry was used to map an Iron Age hillfort in the UK, revealing the defensive ditches, ramparts, and internal structures.

**V. Challenges and Future Directions:**

A. **Interpretation Complexity:** Interpreting magnetometry data can be complex, as anomalies can result from various factors, including archaeological features, geology, and modern disturbances.

B. **Environmental Conditions:** Weather, soil moisture, and vegetation can affect the quality of magnetometry surveys, making data interpretation challenging under adverse conditions.

C. **Depth Limitations:** Magnetometry is most effective at shallow depths, typically up to 2-3 meters, which can limit its use in some contexts.

D. **Integration with Other Techniques:** Combining magnetometry with other survey methods and archaeological investigations enhances its effectiveness in research.

E. **Continual Technological Advancements:** Ongoing advancements in magnetometer technology offer the potential for higher sensitivity and data resolution, improving the accuracy of subsurface feature detection.

In summary, magnetometry is a transformative method in archaeological prospection, offering a non-invasive means of uncovering and mapping sub-surface archaeological features.

As technology continues to advance and interdisciplinary collaboration expands, magnetometry promises to play an increasingly important role in reshaping our understanding of ancient civilizations and their material remains, ensuring that our cultural heritage is preserved for future generations.

# CHAPTER 29: ARCHAEOLOGICAL REMOTE SENSING IN URBAN AREAS

The use of remote sensing technology in archaeology has opened up new frontiers in the exploration and preservation of historical sites and landscapes, especially in urban areas. Archaeological remote sensing in urban environments presents a unique set of challenges and opportunities. This comprehensive exploration will delve into the methods, applications, case studies, challenges, and the transformative impact of remote sensing in uncovering hidden archaeological treasures within the bustling contexts of cities and towns.

## I. Methods and Techniques:

A. **LiDAR (Light Detection and Ranging):** LiDAR technology, with its ability to create highly detailed 3D models of the Earth's surface, is a valuable tool for urban archaeological exploration. It can reveal hidden features like buried structures, ancient streets, and even subsurface utility lines.

B. **Aerial Photography and Satellite Imagery:** Aerial and satellite imagery provide an overview of the urban landscape, allowing archaeologists to identify potential archaeological features, such as ancient roads, city walls, or previously unknown structures.

C. **Multispectral and Hyperspectral Imaging:** These techniques offer insights into material composition, enabling the identification of archaeological features and materials that might be concealed within the urban environment.

D. **Ground-Penetrating Radar (GPR):** GPR can penetrate the urban subsurface, revealing buried structures and artifacts, even in densely built areas.

## II. Applications in Urban Archaeology:

A. **Site Documentation and Mapping:** Remote sensing aids in documenting the urban archaeological landscape, allowing for the creation of detailed maps and 3D models of historical sites.

B. **Cultural Heritage Conservation:** Urban areas often contain historical buildings, monuments, and archaeological sites. Remote sensing assists in monitoring the condition of these structures, enabling conservation efforts.

C. **Archaeological Prospection:** Archaeological prospection in urban environments is challenging due to limited access for traditional excavations. Remote sensing allows researchers to locate and evaluate archaeological remains non-invasively.

D. **Reconstruction of Historical Urban Layouts:** By employing remote sensing, archaeologists can reconstruct the layouts of ancient cities, their streets, buildings, and infrastructure.

E. **Assessing Urban Development Impact:** Urban expansion and construction can impact archaeological sites. Remote sensing helps assess and mitigate the potential harm to cultural heritage.

## III. Case Studies:

A. **Pompeii, Italy:** Pompeii, an ancient Roman city buried by the eruption of Mount Vesuvius, is a classic example of archaeological remote sensing in urban areas. LiDAR and GPR have been used to map the city's layout, identify buried structures, and understand the impact of volcanic ash and lava flows.

B. **Cairo, Egypt:** In Cairo, remote sensing techniques, including multispectral imaging, have aided in locating hidden archaeological features within a densely populated urban landscape, offering insights into the city's long history.

C. **Athens, Greece:** Athens, with its rich archaeological heritage, has benefited from aerial photography and LiDAR to uncover ancient structures and urban planning, shedding light on the development of one of the world's most famous cities.

## IV. Challenges in Urban Archaeology:

A. **Urbanization and Development:** The rapid growth of urban areas often leads to the destruction or disturbance of archaeological sites before they can be studied.

B. **Data Interpretation:** Understanding the complex urban landscape and identifying archaeological features from remote sensing data can be challenging.

C. **Legal and Ethical Issues:** Urban archaeological sites are subject to various legal and ethical considerations, including property rights and cultural heritage preservation.

D. **Cost and Access:** Conducting remote sensing surveys in urban areas can be costly, and gaining access to private properties for data collection may be challenging.

## V. Future Directions:

A. **3D Urban Modeling:** The integration of remote sensing data with 3D modeling techniques will provide more immersive urban reconstructions.

B. **Community Engagement:** Involving local communities and raising awareness about the importance of urban archaeological heritage is crucial.

C. **Sustainable Urban Development:** Remote sensing should play a role in shaping urban planning to minimize the impact on archaeological resources.

In conclusion, archaeological remote sensing in urban areas is a multidisciplinary endeavor that leverages cutting-edge technology to uncover the secrets of our historical urban environments. As urbanization continues to reshape the world, the role of remote sensing in preserving, documenting, and understanding our urban past becomes increasingly vital. Balancing the demands of modern cities with the preservation of our cultural heritage is a challenge, but with remote sensing, we have a powerful tool to navigate this delicate balance and unveil the hidden histories of our urban landscapes.

# CHAPTER 30: DRONES FOR CULTURAL HERITAGE MONITORING

Unmanned Aerial Vehicles (UAVs), commonly known as drones, have revolutionized the way we monitor and preserve cultural heritage. These versatile devices have opened up new opportunities for archaeologists, conservators, and heritage professionals to document, protect, and study cultural heritage sites and artifacts. In this extensive exploration of drones for cultural heritage monitoring, we will delve into the fundamental principles, methods, applications, case studies, challenges, and the transformative impact they have had on the preservation and understanding of our cultural heritage.

**I. Fundamental Principles:**

A. **What is Cultural Heritage?** Cultural heritage encompasses tangible and intangible assets that hold cultural, historical, and artistic significance. It includes monuments, artifacts, archaeological sites, artworks, traditions, and more.

B. **Importance of Cultural Heritage:** Cultural heritage plays a crucial role in preserving the collective memory of societies, fostering identity, and promoting historical and artistic understanding.

C. **Challenges to Preservation:** Cultural heritage is often at risk due to natural disasters, environmental degradation, urbanization, vandalism, and looting.

D. **Non-Invasive Monitoring:** Drones are non-invasive tools for monitoring and documenting cultural heritage, minimizing the risk of damage to artifacts and sites.

**II. Methods and Data Acquisition:**

A. **Types of Drones:** Different drones are used for various purposes, including quadcopters, hexacopters, and fixed-wing drones. They can be equipped with a variety of sensors and cameras.

B. **Photography and Videography:** Drones capture high-resolution photographs and videos of cultural heritage sites and artifacts, providing detailed visual records.

C. **Thermal Imaging:** Thermal cameras on drones can detect temperature variations on artifacts or buildings, revealing hidden features or structural issues.

D. **LiDAR Scanning:** LiDAR-equipped drones create precise 3D models of heritage sites, enabling detailed analysis of their topography and structures.

E. **Multispectral and Hyperspectral Imaging:** These sensors on drones help identify features not visible to the naked eye, such as crop marks or material composition.

**III. Applications of Drones for Cultural Heritage Monitoring:**

A. **Site Mapping and Documentation:** Drones create high-resolution maps and 3D models of cultural heritage sites, enhancing documentation and analysis.

B. **Conservation and Preservation:** Monitoring the condition of heritage sites and artifacts helps conservators identify and address issues, ensuring long-term preservation.

C. **Archaeological Excavation Support:** Drones aid in surveying and documenting archaeological excavations, improving data collection and analysis.

D. **Public Engagement:** Drones provide a unique perspective on cultural heritage that can be shared with the public through virtual tours and educational initiatives.

E. **Landscape and Environmental Studies:** Drones assist in understanding the environmental context of cultural heritage sites, including their interaction with natural surroundings.

**IV. Case Studies:**

A. **Machu Picchu, Peru:** Drones have been used to document and monitor the conservation of the iconic Machu Picchu, providing valuable insights into the site's condition and structural stability.

B. **Pompeii, Italy:** Drones have helped researchers assess the condition of the ancient city of Pompeii, identifying areas in need of urgent preservation.

**V. Challenges and Future Directions:**

A. **Regulatory Compliance:** Navigating the regulatory landscape for drone usage, which varies by country, can be challenging for cultural heritage professionals.

B. **Data Management and Storage:** Handling the large volumes of data generated by drones and ensuring its long-term accessibility and integrity are crucial.

C. **Interdisciplinary Collaboration:** Collaboration between heritage professionals, drone operators, and data analysts is essential for effective drone-based monitoring.

D. **Public Perception:** Public concerns about privacy and the impact of drones on heritage sites must be addressed through education and responsible usage.

E. **Continual Technological Advancements:** As drone technology evolves, new sensors, automated flight planning, and data processing tools will enhance their capabilities for cultural heritage monitoring.

In summary, drones have transformed the way we monitor and preserve cultural heritage, offering non-invasive, cost-effective, and highly detailed methods for documenting and conserving our cultural treasures. As technology continues to advance, and as interdisciplinary collaboration expands, the future of drones in cultural heritage monitoring promises to play an increasingly important role in reshaping how we preserve and understand our shared history and artistic legacy.

# CHAPTER 31: REMOTE SENSING AND CLIMATE CHANGE IMPACTS

Climate change is one of the most pressing challenges of our time, with far-reaching consequences for the environment, ecosystems, and human societies. Remote sensing, the collection of information about the Earth's surface from a distance, has emerged as a vital tool for monitoring and understanding the impacts of climate change. In this comprehensive exploration of remote sensing and climate change impacts, we will delve into the fundamental principles, methods, applications, case studies, challenges, and the transformative role it plays in addressing this global crisis.

## I. Fundamental Principles:

A. **What is Climate Change?** Climate change refers to long-term shifts in temperature, weather patterns, and other climate parameters, often driven by human activities, such as greenhouse gas emissions.

B. **Importance of Monitoring Climate Change:** Understanding the impacts of climate change is essential for mitigating its effects, adapting to new conditions, and making informed policy decisions.

C. **Remote Sensing in Climate Monitoring:** Remote sensing involves using satellites, aircraft, drones, and ground-based sensors to collect data on the Earth's climate system, such as temperature, precipitation, ice cover, and vegetation.

D. **Data Collection and Analysis:** Remote sensing data is collected in various forms, including imagery, temperature measurements, and spectral information, which is then analyzed to detect climate change indicators.

## II. Methods and Data Acquisition:

A. **Satellite Remote Sensing:** Satellites orbiting the Earth capture data on various climate parameters, including sea surface temperatures, ice cover, and atmospheric conditions.

B. **Land-Based Remote Sensing:** Ground-based sensors and weather stations monitor local climate conditions, contributing to the broader understanding of climate change.

C. **Airborne Remote Sensing:** Aircraft equipped with remote sensing instruments provide detailed data on climate parameters, especially for targeted research missions.

D. **Multi-Sensor Integration:** Combining data from multiple sensors and sources enhances the accuracy of climate change monitoring.

E. **Data Assimilation and Models:** Remote sensing data is integrated into climate models to improve predictions and understand the causes and consequences of climate change.

**III. Applications of Remote Sensing in Climate Change Impacts:**

A. **Glacier and Ice Monitoring:** Satellite imagery and remote sensing data track the retreat of glaciers and the loss of ice cover in polar regions, vital for sea-level rise predictions.

B. **Temperature and Precipitation Patterns:** Remote sensing provides information on temperature and precipitation changes, helping understand regional climate shifts.

C. **Vegetation and Ecosystem Health:** Spectral data from remote sensing helps monitor the health of ecosystems and detect changes in vegetation cover due to climate change.

D. **Sea-Level Rise and Coastal Erosion:** Satellite data is critical for assessing sea-level rise and its impact on coastal areas, where populations are vulnerable to inundation.

E. **Natural Disasters:** Remote sensing assists in monitoring and assessing the aftermath of climate-related natural disasters, such as hurricanes, floods, and wildfires.

F. **Carbon and Greenhouse Gas Monitoring:** Satellites and ground-based sensors track atmospheric concentrations of carbon dioxide and other greenhouse gases, aiding climate modeling.

**IV. Case Studies:**

A. **Arctic Sea Ice Decline:** Satellite data has documented the substantial decline in Arctic Sea ice, a direct consequence of global warming, which has wide-reaching environmental and geopolitical implications.

B. **Amazon Rainforest Deforestation:** Remote sensing helps monitor deforestation in the Amazon, which affects global climate due to its role as a carbon sink and regulator of rainfall patterns.

**V. Challenges and Future Directions:**

A. **Data Quality and Validation:** Ensuring the accuracy and reliability of remote sensing data is a continual challenge, requiring calibration and validation efforts.

B. **Data Accessibility and Sharing:** Data should be openly accessible to researchers and decision-makers for informed policy and adaptation strategies.

C. **Integration with In-Situ Observations:** Combining remote sensing with ground-based observations enhances the accuracy and reliability of climate change assessments.

D. **Capacity Building and Training:** Efforts are needed to build local and global capacity for utilizing remote sensing data for climate change research and adaptation planning.

E. **Technological Advancements:** Ongoing developments in remote sensing technology, including improved sensors, higher-resolution imagery, and data processing algorithms, hold promise for more accurate and detailed climate change monitoring.

In summary, remote sensing is a transformative tool in

understanding and addressing the impacts of climate change. By providing extensive and high-quality data, it enables scientists, policymakers, and society to assess the consequences of climate change and take necessary steps to mitigate and adapt to the new reality. As technology continues to advance and interdisciplinary collaboration expands, remote sensing promises to play an increasingly important role in reshaping our understanding of the Earth's changing climate and the urgent need for climate action.

# CHAPTER 32: SATELLITE-BASED ARCHAEOLOGICAL SURVEYS

Archaeology is a discipline that continuously evolves, integrating new technologies and methodologies to enhance our understanding of the past. Satellite-based archaeological surveys represent one of the most innovative and transformative approaches to the field. By leveraging satellite imagery, remote sensing, and Geographic Information Systems (GIS), archaeologists can explore and document archaeological sites, landscapes, and features on a regional or even global scale. In this comprehensive exploration of satellite-based archaeological surveys, we will delve into the fundamental principles, methods, applications, case studies, challenges, and the transformative impact this technology has had on archaeological research.

**I. Fundamental Principles:**

A. **Archaeological Survey Methods:** Traditionally, archaeologists have conducted surveys on the ground, which can be time-consuming and limited in scope. Satellite-based surveys provide a broader perspective, covering vast areas efficiently.

B. **Satellite Imagery:** Satellite imagery, collected by orbiting satellites, serves as the primary data source. This imagery can be captured in various spectral bands, including visible, near-infrared, thermal, and radar.

C. **Remote Sensing Techniques:** Remote sensing involves the collection and interpretation of data about the Earth's surface from a distance. Satellite-based archaeological surveys utilize remote sensing for data acquisition.

D. **GIS Integration:** Geographic Information Systems (GIS) are essential for the management, analysis, and visualization of satellite-derived data in the context of archaeological research.

**II. Methods and Data Acquisition:**

A. **Types of Satellites:** Various types of satellites are used in archaeological surveys, including optical, radar, and multispectral satellites. These capture different types of information, such as visual images, terrain elevation, and land cover.

B. **Satellite Orbits:** Satellites can have different orbits, including polar orbits (which cover the entire globe), sun-synchronous orbits (which provide consistent lighting conditions), and geostationary orbits (which focus on specific regions).

C. **Resolution and Image Interpretation:** The spatial resolution of satellite imagery affects the level of detail that can be observed. Archaeologists interpret these images to identify potential archaeological features.

D. **Data Processing:** Once collected, satellite imagery is processed to enhance specific features or characteristics. This can include the use of image filters, spectral analysis, and data fusion.

E. **Integration with Ground Data:** Satellite-based surveys are often combined with ground-based data, such as geophysical surveys, field observations, and excavations, to verify and validate findings.

**III. Applications of Satellite-Based Archaeological Surveys:**

A. **Site Identification and Mapping:** Satellite imagery is used to identify archaeological sites, document their locations, and create maps for research and management.

B. **Monitoring and Preservation:** Monitoring changes in archaeological sites, particularly those threatened by natural or human factors, helps in their preservation and protection.

C. **Landscape Analysis:** Satellite-based surveys assist in understanding ancient landscapes, including settlements, agricultural systems, and trade routes.

D. **Remote or Inaccessible Areas:** In regions with limited access or security concerns, satellite-based surveys provide a safe and effective means of archaeological exploration.

E. **Contextual Studies:** Archaeologists use satellite imagery to study the context of archaeological sites within their larger landscapes, shedding light on ancient human-environment interactions.

**IV. Case Studies:**

A. **Angkor Wat, Cambodia:** Satellite imagery has been crucial in revealing the vast urban complex of Angkor Wat and tracking its changing landscape over time.

B. **Nasca Lines, Peru:** Satellite surveys have enhanced the study of the enigmatic Nasca Lines, allowing for a broader understanding of these geoglyphs.

**V. Challenges and Future Directions:**

A. **Data Accessibility:** Ensuring access to high-quality satellite imagery is crucial, as some data may be restricted or costly.

B. **Interpretation Complexity:** Archaeological interpretation of satellite imagery can be challenging and may require ground verification.

C. **Environmental and Atmospheric Conditions:** Cloud cover, seasonal changes, and atmospheric interference can affect the quality and availability of satellite imagery.

D. **Integration with Ground Data:** The relationship between satellite-derived data and on-the-ground archaeological research should be well-established to ensure the accuracy of findings.

E. **Continual Technological Advancements:** Ongoing developments in satellite technology, such as higher resolution and more spectral bands, promise to enhance the capabilities of satellite-based archaeological surveys.

In summary, satellite-based archaeological surveys are transforming the field by providing a broader, more efficient means of identifying, documenting, and understanding archaeological sites and landscapes. As technology continues to advance and interdisciplinary collaboration expands, the future of satellite-based archaeological surveys promises to play an increasingly pivotal role in reshaping our understanding of ancient civilizations and their environments, while also aiding in the preservation of our shared cultural heritage.

# CHAPTER 33: THE ROLE OF LIDAR IN FOREST ARCHAEOLOGY

LiDAR, which stands for Light Detection and Ranging, is a cutting-edge remote sensing technology that has significantly impacted the field of forest archaeology. Forests can be challenging environments for archaeological exploration due to their dense vegetation and difficult terrain. However, LiDAR technology has made it possible to uncover hidden archaeological features, study ancient landscapes, and gain a deeper understanding of human interaction with forested areas. In this extensive exploration of the role of LiDAR in forest archaeology, we will delve into the fundamental principles, methods, applications, case studies, challenges, and the transformative impact it has had on archaeological research in wooded environments.

## I. Fundamental Principles:

A. **What is LiDAR?** LiDAR is a remote sensing technology that uses laser pulses to measure distances and generate highly detailed 3D models of the Earth's surface.

B. **Challenges in Forest Archaeology:** Forests often conceal archaeological sites and features under layers of vegetation and soil, making traditional survey methods time-consuming and less effective.

C. **LiDAR in Archaeology:** LiDAR technology can penetrate the forest canopy, providing detailed topographical information and revealing previously hidden archaeological features.

D. **Interdisciplinary Collaboration:** LiDAR application in forest archaeology often involves collaboration between archaeologists, remote sensing experts, and geographers.

## II. Methods and Data Acquisition:

A. **LiDAR Systems:** Airborne LiDAR systems are commonly used for forest archaeology. These systems are mounted on aircraft or drones and emit laser pulses that bounce off the ground and objects on the forest floor.

B. **Point Cloud Data:** LiDAR data is collected in the form of point clouds, which represent the precise location of laser returns. These points create a detailed 3D model of the forested area.

C. **Data Processing:** LiDAR data is processed to filter out noise and vegetation, allowing archaeologists to focus on the ground surface and the potential archaeological features it reveals.

D. **Digital Elevation Models (DEMs):** LiDAR-derived DEMs provide high-resolution topographic information, enabling archaeologists to identify subtle variations in the forest floor.

E. **Data Fusion:** LiDAR data is often combined with other sources, such as satellite imagery, to provide a comprehensive view of the forested landscape.

**III. Applications of LiDAR in Forest Archaeology:**

A. **Site Discovery and Mapping:** LiDAR technology helps identify and map archaeological sites, including ancient settlements, roads, and fortifications hidden in forests.

B. **Revealing Forested Landscapes:** LiDAR data aids in the reconstruction of ancient forested landscapes, providing insights into land use, agricultural practices, and resource management.

C. **Forest Road Networks:** LiDAR reveals ancient road networks and trade routes that may be obscured by dense vegetation, allowing for an understanding of past connectivity.

D. **Archaeological Prospection:** LiDAR assists in archaeological prospection by identifying features such as mounds, earthworks, and depressions.

E. **Conservation and Preservation:** By uncovering previously unknown archaeological features, LiDAR data helps with the preservation of forested cultural heritage.

## IV. Case Studies:

A. **Maya Archaeological Discoveries:** LiDAR technology has been used to uncover extensive Maya cities hidden beneath the dense canopy of the Guatemalan jungle, redefining our understanding of Maya civilization.

B. **Prehistoric Monuments in Europe:** LiDAR has helped identify prehistoric monuments, such as henges and burial mounds, in European forests, offering insights into ancient cultural practices.

## V. Challenges and Future Directions:

A. **Data Processing Complexity:** Interpreting LiDAR data for archaeological purposes can be challenging, and specialized software and expertise are required.

B. **Cost and Accessibility:** LiDAR data collection can be expensive, and access to high-quality LiDAR data may be limited, particularly in remote forested areas.

C. **Ground Verification:** LiDAR findings often require on-the-ground verification to confirm archaeological features and their significance.

D. **Interdisciplinary Collaboration:** Efficient collaboration between archaeologists, remote sensing experts, and other specialists is crucial to the success of LiDAR applications in forest archaeology.

E. **Continual Technological Advancements:** As LiDAR technology continues to advance, its applications in forest archaeology will become even more accurate, affordable, and widespread.

In summary, LiDAR has revolutionized forest archaeology by allowing researchers to see through the dense vegetation that often conceals archaeological features. This technology has led to the discovery of previously unknown ancient sites, improved our understanding of ancient forested landscapes, and contributed to the preservation of forested cultural heritage. As technology continues to advance and interdisciplinary collaboration expands, the role of LiDAR in forest archaeology promises to play an increasingly pivotal role in reshaping our understanding of past civilizations and their interactions with wooded environments.

# CHAPTER 34: RADIOMETRIC DATING AND REMOTE SENSING

Radiometric dating and remote sensing are two powerful tools used in geology, archaeology, and earth sciences to determine the ages of geological features and archaeological sites and to gain insights into Earth's history. This detailed exploration focuses on the principles, methods, applications, case studies, challenges, and the synergy between radiometric dating and remote sensing.

## I. Fundamental Principles:

A. **Radiometric Dating:** Radiometric dating is a technique used to determine the age of rocks and minerals by measuring the proportions of specific isotopes in them. The rate of decay of these isotopes is known and provides a clock for dating geological events.

B. **Remote Sensing:** Remote sensing involves collecting data about the Earth's surface or atmosphere from a distance, often using instruments mounted on satellites, aircraft, or drones. It provides valuable information about surface properties and composition.

## II. Radiometric Dating Methods:

A. **Carbon-14 Dating:** Carbon-14 (C-14) dating is used for relatively young samples, mainly in archaeological and environmental sciences. It measures the decay of C-14, which is absorbed by living organisms and decays after death.

B. **Potassium-Argon Dating:** Potassium-argon (K-Ar) dating is used for dating ancient volcanic rocks. It relies on the decay of potassium-40 to argon-40.

C. **Uranium-Series Dating:** Uranium-series dating includes methods like uranium-thorium and uranium-lead dating, which are used for dating carbonate deposits, cave formations, and rocks.

D. **Luminescence Dating:** Luminescence dating measures the trapped electrons in minerals such as quartz and feldspar to determine when they were last exposed to sunlight or heat.

## III. Remote Sensing Techniques:

A. **Satellite Imagery:** Satellite imagery captures visible and non-visible light, allowing for the study of land cover, vegetation, and geological features.

B. **LiDAR:** LiDAR technology uses laser pulses to create detailed 3D models of the Earth's surface, which can be used to analyze geological and archaeological features.

C. **Hyperspectral Imaging:** Hyperspectral sensors capture information across many narrow, contiguous spectral bands, revealing material composition and mineral content.

D. **Thermal Imaging:** Thermal infrared sensors detect temperature variations on the Earth's surface, aiding in the identification of geological features.

## IV. Synergy between Radiometric Dating and Remote Sensing:

A. **Contextual Information:** Remote sensing provides a broader context for geological and archaeological sites, aiding in the selection of suitable samples for radiometric dating.

B. **Site Discovery:** Remote sensing can identify potential archaeological sites by highlighting surface anomalies or landscape features that may contain datable materials.

C. **Dating Verification:** Radiometric dates can be used to verify the age of features detected through remote sensing, providing a robust chronological framework for geological and archaeological events.

D. **Environmental Changes:** Combining radiometric dating with remote sensing can help track geological processes and the effects of environmental changes over time.

## V. Applications and Case Studies:

A. **Mayan Civilization and LiDAR:** LiDAR technology was instrumental in revealing the extent and complexity of the ancient Maya civilization in the dense jungles of Central America.

B. **Hyperspectral Imaging in Geological Surveys:** Hyperspectral imaging has been used to map and analyze geological formations, mineral deposits, and changes in land cover.

C. **Radiometric Dating of Archaeological Sites:** Radiometric dating has provided precise dates for archaeological sites, confirming historical timelines and revising our understanding of ancient cultures.

## VI. Challenges and Future Directions:

A. **Cost and Access:** Both radiometric dating and remote sensing can be expensive, limiting their application in some research projects.

B. **Interdisciplinary Collaboration:** Collaboration between geologists, archaeologists, remote sensing experts, and environmental scientists is crucial for effective research.

C. **Data Integration and Analysis:** Combining radiometric and remote sensing data requires advanced analytical tools and expertise.

D. **Data Interpretation:** Interpreting remote sensing data and radiometric dates necessitates a deep understanding of the geological and environmental context.

E. **Advancements in Technology:** Ongoing technological advancements in remote sensing and radiometric dating will continue to enhance their capabilities and accuracy.

In summary, radiometric dating and remote sensing are invaluable tools for understanding the Earth's history and uncovering archaeological and geological mysteries. Their synergy allows researchers to gain a more comprehensive understanding of past events and environments, opening new avenues for scientific exploration and discovery. As technology evolves and interdisciplinary collaboration expands, the future of radiometric dating and remote sensing promises to play an increasingly pivotal role in reshaping our understanding of Earth's past and the ancient civilizations that inhabited it.

# CHAPTER 35: CULTURAL HERITAGE MANAGEMENT WITH GIS

Cultural heritage, comprising historical sites, artifacts, monuments, and intangible traditions, holds immense value for society. Effectively managing and preserving this heritage requires the use of innovative tools and methodologies. Geographic Information Systems (GIS) has emerged as a critical technology in the field of cultural heritage management. In this extensive exploration, we will delve into the fundamental principles, methods, applications, case studies, challenges, and the transformative impact of using GIS in managing and preserving cultural heritage.

## I. Fundamental Principles:

A. **Cultural Heritage Management:** Cultural heritage management encompasses activities related to the protection, conservation, research, interpretation, and promotion of cultural resources.

B. **GIS as a Decision Support System:** GIS is a system designed to capture, store, analyze, manage, and present spatial or geographic data. It is a powerful tool for making informed decisions about the preservation of cultural heritage.

C. **Spatial Data Integration:** GIS integrates various types of spatial data, such as maps, satellite imagery, and archaeological surveys, to provide a comprehensive view of the cultural heritage landscape.

D. **Interdisciplinary Collaboration:** Effective cultural heritage management with GIS often involves collaboration between archaeologists, conservators, historians, geographers, and GIS specialists.

## II. Methods and Data Acquisition:

A. **Data Collection and Survey:** Cultural heritage data, including the locations of archaeological sites, historical buildings, and artifacts, are collected through surveys, excavation, and archival research.

B. **Spatial Data Sources:** GIS uses various sources, such as satellite imagery, LiDAR, and aerial photography, to acquire spatial data for mapping and analysis.

C. **Geodatabases:** Geodatabases are used to store and manage cultural heritage data, allowing for efficient retrieval and analysis.

D. **Data Analysis:** GIS tools enable the spatial analysis of heritage data, such as identifying trends in heritage sites' distribution or assessing the impact of environmental factors.

**III. Applications of Cultural Heritage Management with GIS:**

A. **Site Documentation and Inventory:** GIS is used to create detailed inventories and maps of cultural heritage sites, ensuring that they are appropriately documented.

B. **Risk Assessment and Conservation Planning:** GIS helps assess the risks to cultural heritage sites, such as natural disasters or urban development, and formulate conservation strategies.

C. **Public Engagement and Education:** GIS is utilized to create interactive maps and virtual tours, making cultural heritage accessible to the public and promoting education and tourism.

D. **Monitoring and Restoration:** GIS tools assist in monitoring the condition of cultural heritage sites and planning restoration efforts.

E. **Spatial Analysis for Research:** GIS is employed to analyze the spatial distribution of artifacts, monuments, and settlements, shedding light on historical patterns.

**IV. Case Studies:**

A. **Angkor Wat, Cambodia:** GIS has played a vital role in the documentation, preservation, and study of the Angkor Wat temple complex.

B. **Pompeii, Italy:** The use of GIS in Pompeii has facilitated the mapping of archaeological features and the assessment of their conservation needs.

**V. Challenges and Future Directions:**

A. **Data Quality and Accessibility:** Ensuring the accuracy of cultural heritage data and making it accessible is essential.

B. **Interdisciplinary Collaboration:** Facilitating collaboration between heritage professionals and GIS specialists is crucial for effective cultural heritage management.

C. **Data Integration and Standardization:** Efforts are needed to standardize data formats and develop data integration protocols for heritage management.

D. **Public Engagement:** Promoting public awareness and engagement in cultural heritage conservation remains a challenge.

E. **Advancements in Technology:** Continual technological advancements in GIS, including real-time monitoring and advanced data visualization, will enhance cultural heritage management.

In conclusion, GIS has become an indispensable tool in cultural heritage management. Its ability to integrate, analyze, and visualize spatial data allows for more effective planning, preservation, and promotion of our cultural heritage. As technology continues to advance and interdisciplinary collaboration expands, GIS promises to play an increasingly pivotal role in reshaping how we manage and engage with our rich cultural legacy, ensuring it is preserved for future generations.

# CHAPTER 36: ADVANCED REMOTE SENSING TECHNIQUES IN ARCHAEOLOGY

Archaeology, the study of the human past through the examination of material remains, has seen a transformation in recent years with the advent of advanced remote sensing techniques. These technologies have expanded the possibilities of archaeological research by providing new ways to discover, document, and analyze archaeological sites and landscapes. In this comprehensive exploration, we will delve into the fundamental principles, methods, applications, case studies, challenges, and the transformative impact of advanced remote sensing techniques in archaeology.

## I. Fundamental Principles:

A. **Evolution of Remote Sensing:** Remote sensing techniques in archaeology have evolved from traditional aerial photography to more advanced technologies, including LiDAR, multispectral imaging, thermal imaging, and ground-penetrating radar.

B. **Non-Invasive Exploration:** One of the fundamental principles of advanced remote sensing in archaeology is the non-invasive nature of these techniques, which minimize the need for physical excavation and potential damage to sites.

C. **Interdisciplinary Approach:** Archaeologists work alongside experts in remote sensing, geospatial analysis, and geophysics to leverage these technologies effectively.

## II. Methods and Data Acquisition:

A. **LiDAR (Light Detection and Ranging):** LiDAR technology uses laser pulses to create highly detailed 3D models of the Earth's surface, allowing for the identification of subtle topographical features, such as ancient roads, settlements, and terraces, often hidden beneath dense vegetation.

B. **Multispectral and Hyperspectral Imaging:** These techniques involve capturing information across multiple spectral bands, revealing features not visible to the naked eye. Multispectral and hyperspectral sensors can be mounted on satellites, drones, or aircraft.

C. **Thermal Imaging:** Thermal infrared sensors detect temperature variations on the Earth's surface, aiding in the identification of buried features, such as walls and structures.

D. **Ground-Penetrating Radar (GPR):** GPR technology sends radar pulses into the ground and records the reflections, allowing for the detection of subsurface archaeological features.

### III. Applications of Advanced Remote Sensing Techniques in Archaeology:

A. **Site Discovery and Mapping:** These techniques have facilitated the identification and mapping of archaeological sites, sometimes hidden beneath the ground or dense vegetation.

B. **Landscape Analysis:** Advanced remote sensing helps in the reconstruction and analysis of ancient landscapes, such as identifying ancient agricultural systems, terraces, and land use patterns.

C. **Conservation and Preservation:** These technologies assist in monitoring the condition of archaeological sites, helping conservators address issues that may threaten their preservation.

D. **Archaeological Prospection:** Advanced remote sensing techniques aid in archaeological prospection, the process of locating and evaluating buried archaeological remains.

E. **Public Engagement and Education:** These technologies provide the basis for virtual tours, educational initiatives, and public engagement, making archaeology more accessible to a wider audience.

**IV. Case Studies:**

A. **LiDAR in Maya Archaeology:** LiDAR technology uncovered extensive Maya cities hidden beneath the Guatemalan jungle, redefining our understanding of ancient Maya civilization.

B. **Multispectral Imaging at Archaeological Sites:** Multispectral imaging has revealed previously invisible features, such as ancient roads and field boundaries, at archaeological sites in Europe and the Middle East.

**V. Challenges and Future Directions:**

A. **Data Processing and Analysis:** The volume of data generated by advanced remote sensing techniques can be overwhelming, requiring sophisticated data processing and analysis tools.

B. **Cost and Accessibility:** Access to advanced remote sensing technologies can be costly, limiting their use in some regions and by smaller research projects.

C. **Interdisciplinary Collaboration:** Effective collaboration between archaeologists, remote sensing experts, and data analysts is crucial for successful research.

D. **Data Management:** The storage, management, and long-term accessibility of the extensive datasets generated by these technologies pose challenges.

E. **Continual Technological Advancements:** As these technologies continue to evolve, including improvements in sensors, data processing, and automation, they promise to revolutionize archaeological research further.

In summary, advanced remote sensing techniques have opened up new frontiers in archaeology, enabling the discovery and study of archaeological sites and landscapes with unprecedented detail and accuracy. As technology continues to advance and interdisciplinary collaboration expands, the future of advanced remote sensing in archaeology promises to play an increasingly pivotal role in reshaping our understanding of ancient civilizations and their environments, while also aiding in the preservation of our shared cultural heritage.

# CHAPTER 37: REMOTE SENSING IN HISTORICAL CONTEXTS

Remote sensing, the collection of data about the Earth's surface from a distance, has a rich history in various fields, including archaeology, geology, agriculture, and environmental science. In historical contexts, remote sensing techniques have played a significant role in documenting, understanding, and preserving cultural heritage, archaeological sites, and landscapes. In this extensive exploration, we will delve into the historical context of remote sensing, the evolution of technology, methods, applications, case studies, challenges, and the impact of this technology in understanding history and preserving heritage.

## I. Historical Context:

A. **Early Observations:** Humans have been using remote sensing techniques for centuries, beginning with simple observations of the Earth from vantage points such as hilltops and towers.

B. **Aerial Photography:** The invention of the camera in the 19th century paved the way for aerial photography, which allowed for the first systematic documentation of landscapes and archaeological sites from the air.

C. **Early Satellites:** The launch of the first artificial satellites, such as Sputnik in 1957, marked the beginning of modern remote sensing, offering the possibility of global coverage and continuous data collection.

D. **Digital Revolution:** The advent of digital technology in the late 20th century revolutionized remote sensing, enabling the collection, storage, and analysis of vast amounts of data.

## II. Evolution of Technology:

A. **Aerial Photography:** Early remote sensing involved cameras mounted on aircraft, which captured images of the Earth's surface. These images were often processed and analyzed manually.

B. **Satellite Remote Sensing:** The launch of satellites equipped with sensors expanded the scope of remote sensing. These satellites orbit the Earth and capture data on various aspects, including land cover, temperature, and geological features.

C. **LiDAR Technology:** LiDAR, a laser-based technology, provides high-resolution 3D data, enabling the detection of subtle topographical features, even in densely vegetated areas.

D. **Hyperspectral Imaging:** Hyperspectral sensors capture data across hundreds of narrow spectral bands, allowing for detailed analysis of material composition.

### III. Methods and Data Acquisition:

A. **Aerial Survey:** Aerial photography, often captured using fixed-wing aircraft or drones, is widely used to document landscapes and archaeological sites.

B. **Satellite Imagery:** Satellite sensors capture visible and non-visible light, making it possible to monitor land cover changes, environmental conditions, and more.

C. **LiDAR Data Collection:** LiDAR sensors send laser pulses to the ground and record the reflected data, creating highly detailed 3D models of the Earth's surface.

D. **Hyperspectral Data Acquisition:** Hyperspectral sensors record the electromagnetic radiation reflected from the Earth's surface across multiple spectral bands, revealing material properties.

### IV. Applications in Historical Contexts:

A. **Archaeological Site Documentation:** Remote sensing technologies aid in the documentation and mapping of archaeological sites, facilitating research and preservation efforts.

B. **Cultural Heritage Conservation:** Remote sensing techniques are vital for monitoring the condition of cultural heritage sites, including historical buildings and monuments.

C. **Landscape Reconstruction:** Remote sensing is used to reconstruct ancient landscapes and reveal land use patterns, agricultural systems, and trade routes.

D. **Climate and Environmental Studies:** In historical contexts, remote sensing contributes to the study of environmental changes, such as deforestation and land degradation.

E. **Public Engagement:** The use of remote sensing data in historical contexts contributes to public engagement through virtual tours and educational initiatives.

**V. Case Studies:**

A. **Machu Picchu, Peru:** Remote sensing has been instrumental in the study and preservation of the Machu Picchu archaeological site.

B. **Aerial Photography in World War I:** Aerial photographs taken during World War I have been repurposed to document archaeological sites in the Middle East.

**VI. Challenges and Future Directions:**

A. **Data Management:** The storage, management, and accessibility of vast amounts of remote sensing data pose significant challenges.

B. **Interdisciplinary Collaboration:** Collaboration between historians, archaeologists, remote sensing experts, and data analysts is essential for successful research.

C. **Data Interpretation:** Interpreting remote sensing data in historical contexts requires a deep understanding of historical landscapes and features.

D. **Continual Technological Advancements:** As technology continues to evolve, remote sensing in historical contexts will become more accurate, affordable, and widespread.

In summary, the historical context of remote sensing reveals its evolution from simple observations to cutting-edge technology, playing a significant role in documenting history and preserving heritage. As technology continues to advance and interdisciplinary collaboration expands, remote sensing promises to play an increasingly pivotal role in reshaping our understanding of history and culture while contributing to the preservation of our shared historical legacy.

# CHAPTER 38: FUTURE TRENDS IN ARCHAEOLOGICAL REMOTE SENSING

Archaeological remote sensing has rapidly evolved in recent years, revolutionizing the field of archaeology by enabling researchers to explore, discover, and analyze archaeological sites and landscapes with unprecedented precision. The future of archaeological remote sensing holds exciting possibilities, driven by technological advancements and interdisciplinary collaboration. In this in-depth exploration, we will discuss the emerging trends, challenges, and transformative impact of future developments in archaeological remote sensing.

**I. Advances in Technology:**

A. **Higher Spatial Resolution:** Future remote sensing platforms are likely to provide even higher spatial resolution, enabling archaeologists to detect smaller features and details with greater clarity.

B. **Sensors with More Spectral Bands:** Remote sensing systems equipped with a wider range of spectral bands will enhance material discrimination and facilitate the identification of specific archaeological materials.

C. **Integration of AI and Machine Learning:** Artificial intelligence (AI) and machine learning algorithms will automate the analysis of remote sensing data, accelerating feature detection and classification.

D. **Miniaturization and Portability:** The development of smaller, more portable remote sensing systems will facilitate fieldwork and expand access to remote and challenging terrains.

E. **3D and Real-Time Visualization:** Remote sensing

technologies will increasingly incorporate 3D modeling and real-time data visualization, providing a more immersive and interactive experience for archaeologists and the public.

## II. Multisensor Fusion:

A. **Data Fusion:** The integration of data from multiple remote sensing sensors, such as LiDAR, multispectral, and thermal imaging, will provide a more comprehensive view of archaeological landscapes and sites.

B. **Cross-Platform Synergy:** Combining data from satellites, drones, and ground-based sensors will allow for the simultaneous collection of complementary information, increasing the accuracy and efficiency of archaeological surveys.

## III. Unmanned Systems and Robotics:

A. **Advancements in Drones and UAVs:** Drones and Unmanned Aerial Vehicles (UAVs) will continue to be integral for archaeological remote sensing, becoming more capable, autonomous, and affordable.

B. **Underwater and Underground Robotics:** Submersibles, remotely operated vehicles (ROVs), and ground-based robots will be used for underwater and subsurface archaeological exploration.

## IV. Enhanced Data Processing and Analysis:

A. **Big Data and Cloud Computing:** Archaeological remote sensing generates large datasets. Cloud-based platforms and advanced data processing techniques will streamline data storage, management, and analysis.

B. **Artificial Intelligence (AI) and Machine Learning:** AI algorithms will be increasingly used for image analysis, pattern recognition, and the identification of archaeological features within remote sensing data.

C. **Collaborative Data Sharing:** The archaeological community will promote collaborative data sharing, ensuring that remote sensing data is accessible to researchers worldwide.

**V. Integration with Geospatial Technologies:**

A. **Geographic Information Systems (GIS):** Remote sensing data will be seamlessly integrated with GIS, enabling archaeologists to conduct spatial analysis and create detailed geospatial models of archaeological landscapes.

B. **Virtual and Augmented Reality:** These technologies will enable archaeologists to create immersive, virtual reconstructions of archaeological sites for research and public engagement.

**VI. Citizen Science and Public Engagement:**

A. **Crowdsourcing:** Citizen scientists and the public will play a more active role in analyzing remote sensing data, contributing to archaeological research.

B. **Educational Initiatives:** The use of remote sensing data in classrooms and public outreach programs will promote archaeological education and awareness.

**VII. Environmental and Climate Studies:**

A. **Climate Change Impact Assessment:** Archaeological remote sensing will be used to assess the impact of climate change on archaeological sites and landscapes.

B. **Sustainable Practices:** Remote sensing will aid in the development of sustainable conservation and management strategies for archaeological sites.

**VIII. Preservation and Protection:**

A. **Monitoring and Surveillance:** Remote sensing technology will provide continuous monitoring and surveillance of archaeological sites to deter looting and vandalism.

B. **Rapid Response to Threats:** Advanced remote sensing systems will enable rapid response to natural disasters and emerging threats to archaeological heritage.

## IX. Challenges and Ethical Considerations:

A. **Data Privacy and Ownership:** As remote sensing technology becomes more accessible, there will be increased scrutiny of data privacy and ownership issues.

B. **Environmental Impact:** The deployment of remote sensing systems must consider their environmental impact and potential disruption to fragile ecosystems.

C. **Cultural Sensitivity:** Respecting the cultural significance of archaeological sites and involving local communities in research is paramount.

D. **Data Accessibility:** Efforts must be made to ensure that remote sensing data is accessible to researchers from diverse backgrounds and regions.

In summary, the future of archaeological remote sensing is a landscape of immense potential, offering innovative technological advancements, expanded interdisciplinary collaboration, and exciting opportunities for research, education, and preservation. As technology continues to evolve and the archaeological community embraces these transformative trends, the power of remote sensing in archaeology promises to reshape our understanding of the past while safeguarding our shared cultural heritage.

# CHAPTER 39: ETHICS AND CHALLENGES IN REMOTE SENSING ARCHAEOLOGY

Remote sensing archaeology has significantly transformed how archaeologists discover, document, and analyze archaeological sites and landscapes. While the technological advancements have brought numerous benefits, they have also introduced a set of ethical considerations and challenges. In this comprehensive exploration, we will delve into the ethical concerns and challenges associated with remote sensing archaeology, aiming to strike a balance between advancing our understanding of the past and respecting cultural heritage and ethical principles.

## I. Ethical Considerations:

### A. Cultural Sensitivity:

1. **Cultural Heritage Preservation:** Archaeological sites and artifacts often hold profound cultural significance for indigenous and local communities. Remote sensing researchers must prioritize the preservation and protection of these cultural resources.

2. **Respect for Sacred Sites:** Some archaeological sites are considered sacred, and remote sensing activities must respect the spiritual and religious beliefs associated with these places.

### B. Data Privacy and Ownership:

1. **Rights of Indigenous Peoples:** Indigenous communities may assert ownership rights over archaeological data and may have concerns about the dissemination of sensitive information.

2. **Looting and Plundering:** The availability of high-

resolution remote sensing data can inadvertently lead to looting, as it may reveal the locations of previously unknown archaeological sites.

C. **Collaborative Research:**

1. **Inclusivity:** Ethical considerations include involving local communities and indigenous peoples in the research process, collaborating with them on projects, and sharing the benefits of archaeological discoveries.

2. **Data Sharing:** Researchers should be transparent about their data-sharing practices and engage with local communities to determine who has access to the data and how it will be used.

D. **Environmental Impact:**

1. **Ecosystem Disruption:** Deploying remote sensing equipment can have environmental consequences, disturbing ecosystems and impacting local flora and fauna.

2. **Minimizing Footprints:** Ethical remote sensing archaeology should aim to minimize its environmental impact through responsible deployment and post-survey remediation.

II. **Challenges:**

A. **Data Management:**

1. **Data Volume:** Remote sensing produces vast amounts of data, posing challenges in terms of storage, management, and accessibility.

2. **Data Sharing:** While sharing data is essential for archaeological progress, finding appropriate platforms and strategies for data dissemination is a challenge.

B. **Interdisciplinary Collaboration:**

1. **Diverse Expertise:** Effective collaboration between archaeologists, remote sensing specialists, and local

communities requires navigating diverse skill sets and knowledge bases.

2. **Communication:** Bridging the gap between technical experts and non-technical stakeholders can be challenging, as the language and goals of these groups may differ.

## C. Ethical Guidelines:

1. **Lack of Consensus:** The field of remote sensing archaeology lacks uniform ethical guidelines, and the interpretation of ethical principles can vary.

2. **Global Perspective:** Balancing the interests and concerns of various cultural and ethical perspectives on a global scale can be complex.

## D. Cultural Sensitivity:

1. **Understanding Local Values:** Gaining a deep understanding of the local culture and heritage is essential for conducting ethical remote sensing research.

2. **Mitigating Harm:** Archaeologists must assess the potential harm their research might cause to cultural heritage, local communities, and the environment.

## III. Mitigation and Best Practices:

## A. Ethical Frameworks:

1. **Engagement with Local Communities:** Researchers should engage with local communities and indigenous peoples early in the research process to understand their concerns and interests.

2. **Informed Consent:** Informed consent processes should be implemented when necessary, ensuring that local communities are fully informed and can make decisions about the research.

## B. Data Management and Sharing:

1. **Data Access Policies:** Researchers should establish clear policies for data access and data sharing, ensuring responsible data use.

2. **Data Redaction:** Sensitive data should be redacted or excluded from public dissemination when required to protect cultural heritage.

C. **Environmental Responsibility:**

1. **Environmental Impact Assessments:** Researchers should conduct environmental impact assessments before deploying remote sensing equipment to mitigate potential harm to ecosystems.

2. **Site Protection:** In cases of newly discovered sites, steps should be taken to protect them from looting and vandalism.

**IV. Future Directions:**

A. **Ethical Education:** Ethical considerations in remote sensing archaeology should be integrated into education and training programs for archaeologists and remote sensing experts.

B. **Global Collaboration:** The development of international guidelines and ethical standards can ensure a unified approach to ethical remote sensing practices.

C. **Community Empowerment:** Empowering local communities to be active stakeholders in archaeological research fosters ethical collaboration and preservation.

In conclusion, remote sensing archaeology offers remarkable opportunities for discovery and understanding, but these advancements come with ethical considerations and challenges. To strike a balance between advancing archaeological knowledge and respecting cultural heritage and ethical principles, archaeologists and remote sensing experts must prioritize ethical engagement, collaboration, and responsible data management. The future of remote sensing archaeology should be marked by global collaboration, ethical education, and a commitment to the responsible use of advanced technologies.

# CHAPTER 40: CASE STUDIES IN REMOTE SENSING FOR ARCHAEOLOGICAL EXPLORATION

Remote sensing technologies have revolutionized archaeological exploration by enabling researchers to uncover hidden archaeological features and landscapes. This comprehensive exploration delves into several notable case studies where remote sensing techniques have played a pivotal role in revealing ancient civilizations, discovering lost cities, and shedding light on historical mysteries.

## I. LiDAR Revelations in the Maya World:

The use of LiDAR technology in the dense jungles of Central America, specifically in Guatemala, has dramatically transformed our understanding of the ancient Maya civilization. LiDAR-equipped aircraft conducted surveys over hundreds of square kilometers of the Maya Biosphere Reserve, uncovering thousands of ancient Maya structures hidden beneath the thick canopy. These structures include monumental architecture, roads, and agricultural terraces. The discoveries have redefined the extent and complexity of Maya civilization, challenging previous assumptions about their population and organization.

## II. Angkor Wat Rediscovered:

In Cambodia, Angkor Wat, one of the most iconic archaeological sites in the world, underwent a LiDAR-based survey. This endeavor revealed the extent of the Khmer Empire's urban and hydraulic systems, which were previously hidden beneath the dense forests surrounding the temple complex. LiDAR data unveiled an intricate network of reservoirs, canals, and temple complexes, showcasing the sophistication of Khmer engineering and land-use practices. The findings not only expanded our knowledge of Angkor Wat but also raised questions about the environmental sustainability of past civilizations.

## III. Unearthing Ancient Nazca Lines:

The enigmatic Nazca Lines in southern Peru, etched into the desert floor over a thousand years ago, have long puzzled archaeologists. Satellite and drone imaging have provided new perspectives on these geoglyphs, revealing previously unseen patterns and figures. Advanced image processing techniques have highlighted additional geoglyphs, suggesting that the Nazca Lines were more extensive and varied in purpose than previously thought.

## IV. The City of the Monkey God:

In Honduras, the legend of the "City of the Monkey God" had long captured imaginations. Remote sensing, including LiDAR and aerial surveys, confirmed the existence of a sprawling archaeological site, known as the "White City." The technology allowed archaeologists to map the city's layout, revealing plazas, pyramids, and intricate structures, all hidden beneath the dense Mosquitia rainforest. The site, untouched by looters for centuries, offers a unique opportunity to study a virtually pristine ancient city.

## V. Mystery of Stonehenge and the Hidden Landscape:

Stonehenge, a prehistoric monument in England, has been a subject of fascination for centuries. The application of ground-penetrating radar (GPR) and magnetic surveys has unveiled new insights into Stonehenge's landscape. Researchers have identified buried stone circles and avenues, as well as evidence of ancient structures and activity in the vicinity. These discoveries have contributed to a more comprehensive understanding of the purpose and significance of this iconic monument.

## VI. Rediscovering Egypt's Lost City:

In Egypt, archaeologists used infrared satellite imaging to locate an ancient city near the Valley of the Kings. The city, believed to be over 3,000 years old, was remarkably well-preserved and included residential and industrial areas, streets, and even a bakery with ovens and pottery. This discovery has provided unique insights into the daily life of the ancient Egyptians and their interactions during this period.

## VII. Tracing the Nazca Civilization with Multispectral Imaging:

Multispectral imaging was employed in the Nazca Valley of Peru to explore the remnants of an ancient civilization that predated the Nazca people. These images, collected from an aircraft, revealed the presence of ancient geoglyphs, irrigation canals, and settlements. This technology allowed researchers to study how this earlier culture influenced the famous Nazca Lines and the region's agricultural practices.

## VIII. Aerial Photography Uncovering Roman Ruins:

In the UK, aerial photography has been instrumental in discovering Roman ruins. Aerial surveys revealed a vast complex of Roman buildings, including a Roman villa with well-preserved mosaics, buried beneath a field. The findings expanded our understanding of Roman presence in the region and highlighted the significance of aerial photography in documenting archaeological sites.

These case studies underscore the remarkable impact of remote sensing technologies in archaeological exploration. Whether through LiDAR, satellite imagery, drones, or ground-based radar, these tools have revolutionized our ability to uncover hidden archaeological features and landscapes. As technology continues to advance and interdisciplinary collaboration thrives, it is likely that even more archaeological mysteries will be unraveled in the future. Remote sensing has become an indispensable tool in the archaeologist's toolkit, transforming our understanding of past civilizations and the landscapes they inhabited.

# EPILOGUE

In the final chapters of our journey through the pages of "Remote Sensing Technology for Archaeological Exploration," we have embarked on a remarkable voyage across time and terrain. This book has been a testament to the transformative power of remote sensing technology, a tool that has reshaped the landscape of archaeological exploration. We have witnessed how this cutting-edge technology, driven by innovation and the quest for knowledge, has unveiled the secrets of ancient civilizations, uncovered lost cities, and shed light on historical mysteries.

As we reflect on the discoveries presented in this volume, we are reminded of the invaluable contributions of LiDAR, multispectral and hyperspectral imaging, thermal infrared sensors, ground-penetrating radar, drones, and satellites. These technologies have enabled archaeologists to reach new heights, both literally and figuratively, as they've mapped landscapes, discovered hidden structures, and expanded our understanding of past civilizations.

The case studies that have filled these pages - from the sprawling cities of the Maya in Guatemala to the enigmatic lines etched into the Nazca Desert - have taken us on an incredible journey of revelation and wonder. We've explored the once-lost "City of the Monkey God" in Honduras, uncovered the mysteries of Stonehenge, and delved into the daily life of ancient Egyptians through the rediscovery of a lost city. These stories, among others, have demonstrated the vast potential and importance of remote sensing in archaeology.

Throughout this book, we've also navigated the ethical considerations and challenges that come hand in hand with remote sensing archaeology. As we peer into the past, we are reminded of the profound responsibility that comes with wielding such technological power. Cultural sensitivity, data privacy, and environmental stewardship are not mere ethical considerations but guiding principles that must shape our archaeological endeavors.

We've contemplated the need for inclusive and collaborative research, where local communities and indigenous peoples play an active role in archaeological exploration. The future of this field rests on global collaboration, ethical education, and the responsible use of advanced technologies.

The epilogue of our journey is not an end but a new beginning, a call to action for future archaeologists, remote sensing specialists, and all those who are drawn to the mysteries of the past. The technology we have explored within these pages will continue to evolve, uncovering more secrets and opening new chapters in the history of humankind. As we stand at the crossroads of history and innovation, let us remember that our responsibility is not only to explore but to protect, not only to discover but to understand, and not only to peer into the past but to embrace its lessons for the present and the future.

May the pages of this book be an inspiration to all who follow in our footsteps. For as long as the quest for knowledge endures, so too will the wonders and revelations brought forth by remote sensing technology in the timeless pursuit of archaeological exploration.

The End.

www.ingramcontent.com/pod-product-compliance
Lightning Source LLC
Chambersburg PA
CBHW070810280726

48660CB00015B/186